2009
GUIDE TO
SPECIFICATION

BRITISH COUNCIL
FOR OFFICES
BEST PRACTICE IN
THE SPECIFICATION
FOR OFFICES

CONTENTS

CONTENTS

The theme which I have chosen for my term as President of the BCO is 'Challenging Conventions' and in a year which has seen so much economic upheaval, conventions of the past may no longer apply to the future.

Our office buildings have always had to evolve to meet the changing demands of the workplace. However, many other drivers of change now need to be reflected in the design of office space; climate change, demographics, knowledge working, intensification of use, technological advances and the increasing globalisation of the marketplace.

This new Guide to best practice in the specification of offices has been compiled with contributions from over 90 leading industry professionals, all experts in their field, and it is underpinned by the latest BCO research studies into occupier density, small power loads, thermal comfort and structural stability.

With an eye to the future and the need for regular evaluation, this Guide defines what is best in UK office design today and I commend it to you.

Michael Hussey
Senior Vice President of
the British Council for Offices

Chairman of the British Council
for Offices Annual Conference
2009

NEW STREET SQUARE, LONDON
Photographer: Paul Grundy
Courtesy of Land Securities

"With an eye to the future and the need for regular evaluation, this Guide defines what is best in UK office design today and I commend it to you."

WHY IS THIS FIFTH EDITION OF THE GUIDE IMPORTANT FOR YOU? HOW HAS IT CHANGED?

Four years on from the last edition of the Guide and there have been significant increases in the demands placed upon offices. The key matters that the Guide needs to respond to have remained the same; climate change, occupier need, cost and value. The latter comes into sharper focus with the deepening challenges of the general economy while the pace and impact of the sustainability agenda is the most marked change in the last four years.

Getting this Climate Change Bill into law makes Britain a world leader on climate change policy.

Ed Milliband,
Secretary of State for the Department of
Energy and Climate Change

This Guide retains familiar features: a thought piece considering the future direction for office accommodation; sections on building form, structure, engineering services; and the quick guide to key criteria, albeit updated and amended. Its intent remains as before, to provide and communicate best practice in matters concerning the office sector. It is not a prescriptive document but one that presents informed choices to an industry with many and varied demands.

SO WHAT'S NEW?

The UK is the first country in the world to pass legislation, setting legally binding targets to cut greenhouse gas emissions to 80% of 1990 levels by 2050. Buildings account for about 40% of the world's energy use and in the UK are responsible for approximately 50% of national carbon emissions. With this in mind the importance of the sustainability agenda warrants considerable thought and the matter is explored in some detail. Extra commentary is also provided for areas such as vertical transportation, acoustics, building refurbishment, handover and taxation.

It also recognises that the 'one size fits all' approach
of the past is too restrictive a medium to define what is best
in office design. The guide considers in more detail two
building typologies, one an intensively used and serviced
deep plan, urban city centre office and the other a shallow
plan, more passive building.

In recognition of the rapidly changing demands of our industry,
future updates of the guide will be produced to reflect changes
in design practice. These revisions will be available to members
in electronic format through the BCO's website.

The British property industry is recognised for its innovation and
refinement, and for the skill of its practitioners. The BCO Guide
is recognised to be unique, in that it brings together the whole
sector's knowledge into one document. For those who work
globally, equivalent country models are not available and there is
future potential for the guide to be adapted to
reflect country-specific conditions and to
create international benchmarks.

The technical affairs committee would like
to take this opportunity to thank all those
contributors who have given their time and
knowledge so willingly to this, the latest Guide
to Best Practice.

An intelligent building combines
innovations, technological or not,
with skilful management to
maximise return on investment.

International Symposium on
The Intelligent Building – Toronto

Neil Pennell
Land Securities Group PLC

Geoff Harris
Henderson Global Investors

DRIVER FOR CH

The 2009 edition of the BCO Guide is issued at a
pivotal moment for UK commercial development.
The last property cycle was driven not only by
robust economic growth and high employment,
but also by readily available low cost finance.
A generation of highly sophisticated buildings have
been delivered on the back of historically high
capital values. As occupiers seek to optimise their
use of space, and as the sustainability agenda
finally gets real bite, what steps have to be taken
to ensure viability?

S
ANGE

TALKING POINTS

Sustainability

Business performance

Cost & value

1.0 /

"In th
climate, and with
that environmenta
be factored into th
be important to re
prevailing mindse
different products
ways of working i
future conditions.'

current economic

growing realisation

ssues must also

equation, it will

evaluate the

- to investigate

nd different

nticipation of

1.0 /

1.1

THE VALUE CHALLENGE

Offices have been one of the brightest stars in property development and construction. Over the past four years, office construction expanded by 34% in real terms. In particular, growth in the size and profitability of the UK financial services sector created a ready market for high-quality, flexible office space in cities throughout the UK. New benchmarks for land values, rentals, performance and build quality were set, with many schemes introducing, for the first time, London standards of specification and performance into regional office markets.

With the outlook less certain, the industry as a whole needs to consider the steps that may have to be taken to tailor new development to changed economic circumstances, cost effectively providing space which supports the operation of successful companies, contributes to the wider community, and provides a worthwhile return for developers and long-term investors in a more subdued market.

In the current economic climate, and with a growing realisation that environmental issues must also be factored into the equation, it will be important to re-evaluate the prevailing mindset – to investigate different products and different ways of working in anticipation of future conditions.

RE-THINKING DEVELOPMENT

With the RICS currently forecasting peak-to-trough falls in capital value of over 50%, the starting point for the next development cycle – for both land and construction cost – will need to be significantly below current benchmarks. However, specifications cannot stand still. Occupiers want space that can be occupied at higher densities, and low carbon emission

QUATERMILE ONE, EDINBURGH
Copyright: Foster + Partners
Photographer: Nigel Young

requirements will become increasingly stringent. As a result, the viability debate will be focused on minimising the cost premium of design excellence, build quality, complexity and built-in flexibility – precisely the qualities by which developers have differentiated their product in the current cycle.

Steps taken now to address the 'value challenge', through the adoption of appropriate standards for high-quality but functional office space, will create a product targeted at a subdued, post-boom letting and investment market. In anticipating the eventual recovery of demand, it is prudent to assume that not all sites will boast a combination of location, design and space planning opportunity to achieve significant premiums on either rent or yield – particularly if investment markets remain tight and therefore the focus will have to be upon construction cost.

Where are we now?

Even the least observant visitor to a major UK city could not fail to notice the positive impact of recent large scale office development on the wider urban public realm. Mixed use schemes such as Cardinal Place in London's Victoria, or large scale redevelopments including Spinningfields in Manchester, Quarter Mile in Edinburgh, More London and Kings Cross have an impact and add value well beyond the financial transactions between developer, investors and occupiers.

In addition to investment value defined by rent and yields, value from offices is also being secured by occupiers through operational efficiency and brand association; while other landowners, space users and the general public all benefit from the indirect uplift of a 'rising neighbourhood'; particularly if some of the exchange value is reinvested into public realm or planning gain. However, as investment values fall away, can quality-driven development strategies be maintained?

1.0 /

DRIVERS FOR CHANGE

The current supply side approach presents many opportunities to enhance value and product responsiveness in a challenging market. The opportunities include:

→ **Specification and design.** Expenditure on architectural expressiveness and quality, building capability and flexibility have all driven cost growth during the last development cycle. Regional cities have secured a generation of good quality, flexible office buildings, whereas the central London market has pursued a different type of product, whether tall, iconic

RBS HEADQUARTERS, GOGARBURN, EDINGURGH
Copyright: Keith Hunter

or both, central London office build costs have increased faster than general construction inflation, even though occupiers' standards, as defined by BCO for example, have not changed markedly during the period. The upward trend indicates that over the period, 2004–2009, average London office build costs have increased by up to 10% per annum over and above general inflation. While some of this cost has been driven by regulatory change, or by excess inflation in a very over-heated market, a proportion also reflects an increase in the inherent cost of design. Drivers for discretionary design enhancements will have included a greater commitment to sustainability through higher BREEAM ratings, greater expenditure on public realm and the premium associated with iconic buildings.

→ **Planning and regulatory requirement.** The principle objective of development is to provide modern, efficient and sustainable commercial space. High capital values and the strategic nature of many large development opportunities have enabled planning and regulatory authorities to secure substantial community value, in terms of development quality, planning gain and public realm investment. Few would question the contribution to the wider public good made by developers and investors in the current cycle, although in markets where capital values are continuing to fall, these requirements are less affordable and could potentially stifle redevelopment and the delivery of any benefit whatsoever.

→ **Availability of contractor resources.** After years of scarcity, securing a contractor is less of a challenge, but tailoring the right resources to the project represents a major opportunity. Large scale commercial developers have been exposed to the consequences of 'market failure' during the last 2–3 years, when limits on absolute industry capacity and the number of players in the large project sector combined to produce a seller's market. The shortage of resource was a result of industry consolidation, contractor's supply-chain management practices and the emergence of a new class of mega-project. However, even in the current market, forecast reductions in tender prices are not keeping pace with deteriorating capital values. Affordability is a key aspect of commercial viability and capital cost management is concerned with enabling development to proceed rather than optimising profit. Tailoring project opportunities to the right supply chain has to become a greater priority as developers and contractors face a common future of scarcer workload and potentially lower profitability. Developers should look beyond their settled supply chain to identify whether other contractors might be better configured to deliver the best balance of cost, programme, quality and certainty.

→ **Shared objectives.** The final area of value adding activity concerns teamwork and collaboration – values which are at risk of being set aside as clients consider making more use of price competition to drive cost out of projects and to increase viability. The 'market failure' described above suggests that the experience of clients who took the time to develop long term relationships with their supply chain were mixed. However, whilst there is only limited evidence of the evolution of a culture of mutual interdependence between client and project team, relationships are managed in a far more mature and measured way than they were even 10 years ago. Early return to construction will be facilitated by shared objectives and collaborative working, focused on the allocation and removal of risk, trimming of waste and concentration on design and construction value drivers.

In summary, there are many opportunities in the property development process to add value and take cost out of the development equation. When values are rising, this is less of a priority, but in order to be ready to respond to the return of demand, all project players need to focus on how they can contribute to getting projects across their viability hurdles.

Where should we be going?
An effective and efficient building is typically thought to be suitable for purpose if it is designed to be well matched to the immediate and long-term needs of occupiers and owners. Efficiency is also concerned with being lean – sometimes erroneously associated with strictly functional 'rent slab' architecture, but actually associated with the adoption of standard processes, components and systems in the delivery of high quality.

As developers and their project teams address function and suitability for purpose in a downturn, the risk is that the strides that have been made in raising build quality, reducing environmental impact and contributing to public realm, will also be at risk as the value differentiators of an office design are challenged by round after round of cost-driven value engineering.

Faced with current viability gaps, the approach to development might require a radical step change, but this must not be at the expense of necessary function and operational quality. The bulk of the cost of a commercial office is spent on the substructure, frame and upper floors, external walls, services and contractor's on-costs. If radical changes are going to be made, they must be focused on high cost areas, because incremental change may not be enough.

One of the characteristics of our current commercial architecture has been the emergence of a generation of exceptional, 'iconic' office buildings, designed to secure enhanced planning consents in sensitive and valuable locations. These innovative and inspirational buildings exemplify why overseas designers and specialist contractors like to work in the UK, but equally, they point to the challenges we face in returning to the disciplines of a more modest financial model.

So where should we focus our attention?
In the current downturn, we must take the opportunity to learn from our occupiers and the performance of the buildings we have completed over the last 10–20 years.

→ **Developing the right site.** Highly constrained sites which require complex structural solutions or which impose irregular or inefficient floor plates are best left to later in the upturn when values are higher. Sites with the least inherent risk and cost provide a springboard for fast, simple, low risk development.

→ **Developing the optimum floor area – not the maximum.** Diminishing rates of return can affect schemes which aim for the absolute maximisation of floor area, either due to additional planning requirements or due to physical constraints which the structure, services and envelope have to resolve. Better value may be secured by a lower-cost solution, and appraisals should reflect this potential range of outcomes.

→ **Minimising time in the ground.** Basement construction results in extended programmes and is a high-cost route to delivering low-value space. With the main contractor's management costs representing over 16% of cost, steps taken to reduce project duration will benefit the bottom line. Even large in-town retail schemes are exploring alternatives to basement goods distribution, and office developers should also consider alternatives.

→ **Maximising net-to-gross.** Improving building efficiency makes a vital contribution to a development's bottom line. A change of 5% in net-to-gross ratio, for example 80–85%, could equate to a 14% premium in the cost of net office space, related to efficiency alone. The impact of measures to improve net-to-gross on the layout of the floor plate should be taken into account, but in principle, any measures which maximise rental streams should be pursued.

1.0 /

"Faced with
gaps, the approach to
might require a radica
but this must not be a
necessary function and

current viability
development
step change,
the expense of
operational quality."

→ **Minimising wall-to-floor ratios and slab-to-slab heights.**
Façades are increasingly required to deliver greater levels
of performance, and as a result, costs increase. Projects will
only stack up if we build within a tighter building envelope,
so wall-to-floor ratios have to be optimised. The decrease of
wall-to-floor ratio from 0.50 to 0.40 on a typical city centre
office building could reduce overall build costs by around 5%,
and will also have knock on effects on the extent of perimeter
cooling zones, cleaning costs etc.

→ **Understanding how occupiers use buildings.** Developer
provision for basic occupier requirements such as cooling
and small power loads, air conditioning terminal unit density,
standby power, BMS control and so on, vary significantly.
Despite the best efforts of the BCO, specification standards
are not always based on empirical data concerned with how
buildings are used. In the current downturn, we must take the
opportunity to learn from our occupiers and the performance
of the buildings we have completed over the past 10–20 years.

→ **Completing and coordinating design and construction.**
Project process remains a big opportunity to address waste,
efficiency, cost and risk – even despite all of the investment
in CAD, extranets and so on. Indeed, downtime in the current
market is a good time to review process, albeit not to invest
in new systems. Most players in the supply chain, developers
included, will argue that they have good systems, but the
problem is that they don't integrate well. Best practice studies
show that there are real opportunities for savings from
joined-up collaborative working which could leave some
headroom for some of the building features that project teams
really value. Starting with the coordination of professional
services, the coordination of design, and the use and reuse of
information, how we do things offers plenty of opportunity for
adding to the bottom line.

→ **Simplifying our specifications and adopting standard solutions.** Specialist contractors enjoy working in the UK because they can secure great projects, interesting challenges and profitable opportunities to develop one-off solutions. We are actually very progressive in our use of pre-fabrication and modular components in office construction, but often on the basis of bespoke rather than off-the-peg products. Bespoke solutions inevitably come at a cost, and a shift to a 'mass customisation' must have the potential to deliver similar performance and much better value. Further opportunities abound in fit-out, joinery, metalwork and light fittings. Individually, these components don't represent a significant spend, but even in active markets, highly commoditised products such as ceiling tiles, doors etc. are always subject to downward cost pressure.

→ **Rationalising the site team and ensuring performance.** The effects of the recession are likely to put paid to generously resourced contractors' site teams. Whereas clients have been challenging the extent of management resource and site services, in the future, it will be important to ensure that the logistics required to deliver the programme are in place, rather than those determined by the contractor's competitive tender.

→ **Getting the risk balance right.** It is easier for clients to transfer risk when work is scarce, and the temptation grows when highly competitive bids are being submitted. Clients do have to take measures to ensure that a contract is managed in a way that contractor entitlements to reimbursement do not occur, but should retain a fair risk allocation in the contract. Removing major risks from a principal contract – such as below ground work – can also make a contract more attractive, securing better tenders.

THE WIDER CHALLENGE

The development community's challenge is to create opportunities to deliver modern office space, in turn facilitating an occupiers' effectiveness and contributing positively to the wider community. Decisions made today will have long-term implications for building value; and yet our challenge is set in a rapidly changing and potentially contradictory world.

In summary, as we seek to deliver space into a dynamic and challenging marketplace, there are wider issues that need to be considered, because they could drive long-term value in the wrong direction. Unless a holistic approach is taken, incremental or short-term cost reductions made to meet viability hurdles may deliver inappropriate and unsustainable assets.

The new or evolving challenges we will face are discussed below.

1.2

WHAT DO OCCUPIERS WANT?

For more than 100 years, office buildings have been a familiar part of the urban landscape, whether as iconic city-centre landmarks, or the common-or-garden blocks that line the streets of towns across Britain. But since the turn of the 21st Century there has been a growing awareness that office life is changing – primarily due to the developments in electronic communications technology, but also because we now have a better understanding of the influence that office design can have on the way people work.

A natural consequence of organisations' efforts to minimise overheads will be to work office space harder. Research undertaken by both the BCO and IPD during 2008 has provided plenty of evidence of increasing occupational densities with implications for design and specification. Wider adoption of flexible working patterns could also potentially take place, with

FURTHER READING
BCO Occupier Density
Study, 2009

technology solutions available to address the practical issues –
and more occupiers prepared to address the cultural challenges
in a tougher employment market.

Fundamentally, occupiers need their offices to deliver
three things:
→ Productivity
→ Good value for money
→ Prospect of best place to work.

But for an increasing number of occupiers, there is a fourth
factor to be addressed – they wish their offices to convey a
message, subliminal or blatant, about the underlying ethos of
their organisation, typically in terms of their 'corporate social
responsibility' (CSR) and in order to assist recruitment and
retention of the best people.

ISG HQ, ALDGATE HOUSE, LONDON
Copyright: ISG; Photographer: Richard Leeney

OPTIMUM PRODUCTIVITY

Occupiers know that the cost of people working in an office is far greater than the day-to-day operational costs of running the office (such as providing heat, power, and other services). The logical conclusion is that a small increase in the productivity of those workers could result in substantial overall savings that far outweigh savings in operational energy costs.

There are numerous studies that correlate workplace productivity with building characteristics and indoor environmental quality, and the topic is further discussed in Appendix A5: Business performance. While these studies conclude that, on a case-by-case basis, high-performance buildings improve worker productivity, there is no UK research presenting a large-scale, statistically significant sample of post-occupancy evaluations in real buildings, addressing the number of sick days, occurrence of asthma, staff alertness, and so on.

With recruitment and staff retention generally a key concern for office occupiers, it is essential for employers and investors/ developers to be able to understand and anticipate staff priorities and preferences, in terms of their office environment, if buildings are to enhance productivity.

Figure 1.1 Occupier priorities, courtesy of Savills Research; YouGov

Important to very important (% of respondents)

Comfort
Temperature
Lighting
Length of commute
Noise
Security
Public transport
Car parking
Kitchen
Shops and leisure

0   20   40   60   80   100

It is essential for employers and investors/developers to be able to understand and anticipate staff priorities and preferences, in terms of their office environment, if buildings are to enhance productivity.

Good design should anticipate the needs and desires of occupiers. A report carried out by YouGov towards the end of 2007 provides an interesting insight into the relevant ranking of workplace attributes (see Figure 1.1).

Inevitably location/commute features strongly, but these factors are, surprisingly, secondary to comfort in the working environment – with comfort, lighting and temperature being considered the most important issues. Facilities such as crèche and gym were not rated as having the same level of importance, with around half of those questioned placing no relevance on their availability. Setting issues such as salary and working hours aside the other key element/offer for staff was a clear 'green' agenda/policy with over 61% of interviewees highlighting the issue.

In practice, these issues warrant increased input to ensure flexibility in the design and optimum performance of indoor comfort systems and natural daylight/artificial lighting. Careful consideration needs to be given to the orientation of the building, to maximise daylight and also to give views out. Kitchen facilities are now regarded as standard, but the inclusion of other types of 'break-out' space could become more important, as is the need to cater for a mobile workforce – with hot-desking and 'touch down' points becoming more popular. Options to offer communal break-out space in multi-let buildings could also be an asset, particularly if planned from the outset.

These features will increase initial development costs and occupiers need to recognise this in the premiums that they are prepared to pay if the industry is to continue to develop good quality, flexible and sustainable buildings.

GOOD VALUE FOR MONEY

It is not easy for occupiers to understand whether they are obtaining good value for money from the buildings they rent or own. Data on design performance and actual building performance needs to be public and easily accessible. Only then can occupiers make informed decisions about the type of buildings they would like to use. In addition, publicly available data on energy, water consumption and thermal comfort surveys would also help researchers and legislators draw conclusions about the effectiveness of regulations and voluntary rating systems. This sort of publicly available data is missing at the moment.

The recent introduction of display energy certificates (DECs), currently for public buildings, will improve transparency, at least for energy consumption, and building rating systems such as BREEAM and LEED have already incorporated mandatory post-occupancy evaluation which will provide crucial non-financial insights.

However, the potential of these tools is not yet being adequately realised. A few years will have to pass before there is enough actual resource consumption data from DECs for occupiers and legislators to be able to compare design and in-use figures.

> Publicly available data on energy, water consumption and thermal comfort surveys would help researchers and legislators draw conclusions about the effectiveness of regulations and voluntary rating systems.

THE SOCIAL DIMENSION

Data on energy consumption and from post-occupancy evaluation (POE) studies will only be a partial solution to creating a link between the building provider and the occupier. Although the UK government's and the European Union's long-term strategies concentrate on energy, the business case for high-performance buildings in most cases needs to consider not just energy savings or even straightforward environmental sustainability, but the more abstract concept of 'corporate social responsibility' (CSR).

The YouGov study (Figure 1.1) suggests that a strongly defined environmental policy will influence employees and therefore occupational criteria. Many well-known businesses are also beginning to realise that a strong public commitment to CSR also makes good business sense – and occupying environmentally sensitive and sustainable 'green' buildings is an excellent way to enhance their public image.

Thus, moving forward, these issues will have a significant influence on occupiers' choice.

From the developer's point of view, however, the case is not so clear cut. Inevitably the first questions a developer asks about 'green' buildings are: 'How much is it going to cost me?' and 'Is there a financial advantage?'

For owner-occupiers, the answers to these questions depend on their organisation's long-term vision, and are supported by a number of case studies. Nevertheless, there is evidence that, in the long-term, the benefits outweigh any premium associated with the actual construction of the building itself.

For instance, as reports by Davis Langdon's Lisa Matthiesen and Peter Morris illustrate,[1] green buildings do not have to have an added first cost; yet productivity gains and operational savings are significant, as described in several case studies from the Building Research Establishment (BRE) and the US Green Building Council (USGBC) and other organisations.[2] The maximum premium for green building construction reported in the Davis Langdon studies is 3% to 5%. At the same time, productivity gains of 25% to 30% and operational cost savings of 30% are routinely reported for green buildings.[3]

There are many more equally relevant studies. Suffice to say that, for an owner/occupier with a long-term view and solid operational procedures that help realise the potential cost savings, there is a well-documented business case for green office buildings.

[1] Matthiessen Lisa F, Peter Morris. Costing Green: A Comprehensive Cost Database and Budgeting Methodology, Davis Langdon, July 2004; and Matthiessen Lisa F, Peter Morris. Cost of Green Revisited : Reexamining the Feasibility and Cost Impact of Sustainable Design in Light of Increased Market Adoption, July 2007

[2] Kornevall, C. Energy Efficiency in Buildings: Business Realities and Opportunities, World Business Council for Sustainable Development, October, 2007

[3] Corps, Chris. Green Value : Green buildings, growing assets, Royal Institution of Chartered Surveyors, 2006

For speculative offices, the questions about cost and, especially, about profitability are more difficult to answer. When owner/occupiers decide to develop green office buildings, they are aware of and appreciate the expected cost savings and productivity increases. The speculative office developer, on the other hand, does not know whether the prospective occupiers/buyers will have an appreciation for the benefits of green buildings and, consequently, whether they would be willing to pay a premium for a green building.

Research papers on this issue are few and far between and concentrate on the US commercial real estate market. For instance, the CoStar group – one of the largest sources of commercial real estate information – found that buildings 'rated' under the Energy Star and LEED schemes attract higher rental values and higher occupancy rates, regardless of size, age or location.[4] A similar study by the University of California suggests an effective rental income premium of 4% to 6% – that is, when increased occupancy rates are also taken into account.[5]

Both these studies used statistical modelling to eliminate the effects of building age, location, height, size and class, and compared rental rates with buildings of similar characteristics within a quarter mile radius. Thus the results indicate a rental premium that is a function only of the presence of a 'green' certification and not any other features of the building. On the other hand, these studies were not able to establish whether the rental premiums are a result of predicted cost savings and increased productivity or other attributes of the green label itself (i.e. the market value of the LEED and Energy Star brand).

Similar studies that would examine rental rates as a function of green BREEAM certification in the UK are in progress. Such studies would certainly strengthen the business case for green commercial buildings in the speculative market.

[4] CoStar Group (Miller, N., Spivey, J., and Florance, A.) 'Does Green pay off' in The Journal of Sustainable Real Estate, March, 2008 (www.costar.com/josre/pdfs/costar-JOSRE- Green-Study.pdf)

[5] Eichholtz, P., Kok, N., and Quigley, J. M., Doing Well By Doing Good? Green Office Buildings. Working Paper No. W08-001. University of California. April, 2008

"The full impact of corporate environmental policies is yet to be seen but there is little doubt that the subject will become increasingly important to occupiers."

The full impact of corporate environmental policies is yet to be seen, but there is little doubt that the subject will become increasingly important to occupiers. Historically, design and specification – particularly within the speculative market – has generally paid little more than 'lip service' to the environmental agenda, not helped by long term payback on the majority of viable options. However, the market will inevitably follow more public-sector-based guidelines when considering occupational parameters and, as such, more detailed consideration of delivering cost-effective green solutions will be a fundamental requirement.

1.3

SUCCESSFUL BUILDINGS ARE SUSTAINABLE BUILDINGS

As carbon reduction targets start to bite, and as 'corporate social responsibility' (CSR) rises up boardroom agendas, the mitigation of environmental impacts of buildings and commerce will grow in importance as a differentiator and a cost driver. For most developers, the CSR and environmental agenda became established in the upturn, informed by climate change and new legislation. However, mandatory carbon budgets are likely to affect office occupiers as well as manufacturers, and low carbon specifications could also have implications for the use of buildings, including allowable occupational densities.

In the current uncertain economic climate, it is difficult to know what the future holds. High energy prices are likely, while legislation will inevitably fuel a drive towards lower energy consumption and emissions. Equally, unforeseen changes in technology, or in local or regional weather patterns, could have a dramatic impact on offices within the design life of today's new buildings.

FURTHER READING
Soft Landings:
www.softlandings.org.uk

Global Reporting Initiative:
www.globalreporting.org

In his overview in the 2005 version of this Guide, Rab Bennetts lamented the 'dislocation between the provider of the building and its occupier', remarking that routine post-occupancy checks to assess the building's actual performance are completely missing from the industry's culture.

This information gap will not be adequately addressed by Display Energy Certificates (DECs) or rating systems such as BREEAM or LEED, which mostly concern environmental sustainability. Instead, it is important to monitor building performance over the first 24 months of occupancy, to allow the occupiers to understand the controls and user requirements and make necessary adjustments. It is important to keep in touch with the way the building is used and performs on completion as a continuous learning tool for all parties. Good design will always look at how offices can be operated and maintained over the design life. Schemes such as 'Soft Landings' (a joint initiative between BSRIA, the Usable Buildings Trust and the Darwin Consultancy, which aims to develop a set of procedures and worksteps for project teams to stay engaged with buildings after practical completion) will help with this process. In addition, voluntary CSR tools, such as the Global Reporting Initiative and the ISO 14000 series are a step towards this aim.

If comprehensive data on workplace productivity for real UK office buildings was collected and made publicly available, the business case for investment into high-performance offices could be strengthened. However, data and lessons learnt must be disseminated widely to the industry and potential occupiers. Now more than ever it is essential to learn from experience, and this means that information from post-occupancy studies is needed urgently.

Sustainability is not a stand-alone feature of buildings that can be bolted on, almost as an afterthought. Quite the contrary: it is an all-pervading phenomenon that it is bringing about a revolution in the way we go about the business of designing and building offices.

UNDERSTANDING SUSTAINABILITY

Sustainability is about the careful use of existing resources, coupled with an exhortation to minimise pollution and waste. This would be sensible advice for any business, but it has grown in significance because we now know that the dramatic increase in the use of one particular natural resource – fossil fuels (coal, oil and gas) – since the Industrial Revolution is releasing excessive amounts of greenhouse gases (mainly carbon dioxide) into the atmosphere. This action is driving the process of climate change – the effects of which are already evident and if allowed to continue unchecked will have dramatic consequences for the world's ecosystem.

The construction and operation of buildings accounts for around half of all the UK's carbon emissions, and with international, regional and national governments all setting targets to cut carbon emissions, a 'low carbon' agenda is here to stay.

Cutting carbon emissions, however, is not the only aspect of sustainability that should concern the offices sector. Buildings consume vast quantities of natural resources other than fuel including water, materials (concrete, timber, glass, plastics), both during construction and throughout their life.

Barriers to sustainable offices

There is already plenty of evidence that well-designed, low-carbon, energy-efficient buildings are often more pleasant to occupy and offer significantly lower running costs when compared with conventional buildings. Nevertheless, there are numerous barriers to sustainable 'green' office buildings:

→ **Speculative developments:** Initial investment is by a developer or investor, but the occupier is reaping cost saving and productivity benefits. Today the developer often has to convince the agent, occupier and buyer of the added value of environmental features if it is to recover its initial investment in sustainability measures. There is little proof of the predicted performance improvements so far. Any operational cost benefits from additional capital investment in environmental initiatives need to be shared between developer and occupier if developers are to justify the additional initial build costs. Similarly, savings in cost-in-use achieved by changes in occupiers' behaviour (in relation to minimising the use of resources and reductions in waste) need to be recognised.

→ **Poor understanding:** Can the property realise its 'green' potential? Do occupiers know how to operate/maintain the building? Do they track resource consumption? Are they obliged in some way to maintain the 'green' features of the building and thus maintain its value?

→ **Valuation:** The value of productivity increase is not routinely factored into the return on investment (ROI). For example, the ROI on a purely energy-saving measure, such as insulation, may only be related to the actual expected annual cost saving, but what about the value of carpets chosen for their minimal use of volatile organic compounds (VOCs)?

→ **Accountability:** If the occupier is paying a rental premium, the building should do 'what it says on the tin' (i.e. deliver predicted cost savings, productivity gains, etc).

→ **Demand:** Occupiers and buyers have to keep demanding high-performance buildings in order for developers to build them. Only when the demand side of the commercial office world embraces the cost savings from productivity gains and reduced absenteeism in addition to operational savings, will there be a true business case for green buildings.

The above could be summarised as the 'wait and see' scenario, whereby all parties are waiting for someone else to take the plunge and opt for sustainability, and only a few high-profile – and sometimes experimental – developers or clients have taken up the challenge. This scenario, however, is on the wane, as both national and international pressures begin to take hold.

Drivers for sustainability
In the previous (2005) edition of this BCO Guide, Rab Bennetts
concluded: 'Compulsion through regulation is the only alternative'.

In the relatively short time since then, much has changed:
→ There has been an expansion and tightening of both Building
  Regulations and planning requirements, leading to buildings
  that use far less energy and have a lower impact on the
  environment.
→ The introduction of compulsory Energy Performance
  Certificates (EPCs) throughout the UK during 2008 sent a clear
  signal that the energy performance of buildings is firmly on the
  political agenda.
→ Public and industry awareness of sustainability issues has
  been heightened due to the introduction of various measures,
  such as the government's 'roadmap' to achieving zero carbon
  in all new-build dwelling projects by 2016 and in all other
  new-build projects by 2019.

The UK government is continuing to set mandatory minimum
standards through Building Regulations, and requiring broader
sustainability commitments from developers as part of the
planning process. Overall, although there are differences
between the devolved administrations (due to differences in
the legal systems and climate variations), the 'direction of
travel' is clear.

The single most important piece of UK environmental
sustainability legislation in the past four years is the
implementation of the EU's Energy Performance of Buildings
Directive (EPBD), transposed into UK law in the form of new
Building Regulations and the introduction of Energy Performance
Certificates (EPCs) and Display Energy Certificates (DECs).
Although EPCs and DECs are still relatively new, and the jury
is still out on whether their effects on the market will live up
to expectations, the new Building Regulations have already
firmly shifted attention towards energy use when designing
new buildings.

In addition, local planning policy has been instrumental in promoting renewable energy and community heating schemes for new developments. The policy of mandating new projects to compensate for a portion of their carbon emissions by employing on-site renewables emerged from the London Borough of Merton and is spreading quickly around the country's planning departments. Newly adopted local development framework (LDF) documents are increasingly adopting quantitative renewable energy targets for new developments, ranging from 10% to 20% in most cases.

Voluntary schemes have also developed further since 2005:
→ Eco Homes has been replaced by the Code for Sustainable Homes, and this new Code has been adopted as a mandatory rating system for government-funded housing projects.
→ Although the BREEAM Offices rating system has become more stringent than ever before, an increasing number of projects are achieving a BREEAM rating and BREEAM has truly become a national benchmark for office buildings. BREEAM for offices is still voluntary, but planning departments in urban areas have all but unofficially adopted BREEAM as a required metric for new developments.
→ The US-based LEED system has also recently appeared on the UK market.

If 'sustainability' is meant to encompass social, economic and environmental issues, the building's value should reflect how the building is better in all these areas.

Meanwhile, there are hints of how the social aspects of sustainability will have to be incorporated into building design to a greater extent than today.

Although sustainable buildings are becoming highly desirable, partly because of their superior internal environment, today's valuation methods do not fully take into account the added value from the offer– in the building or beyond the site boundary. If 'sustainability' is meant to encompass social, economic and environmental issues, the building's value should reflect how the building is better in all these areas.

As mentioned, quantifiable data that productivity increases in high-performance buildings is currently very scarce and often not available to the public, so added research and transparency would enable valuers of high-performance buildings to put a price tag on the value of 'green' and communicate the value of sustainability to property investors.

Sustainable offices, with their low-carbon, energy-efficient and socially responsible approach to development, are more likely to comply with future legislation, thus decreasing the risk of premature obsolescence. Furthermore, occupiers keen to demonstrate their environmental commitment will increasingly seek out low carbon buildings, potentially leading to rental premiums.

However, while it is widely recognised that new build construction can move rapidly towards the low- or zero-carbon goal, the greatest challenge we face as a country, and more specifically as an industry, is the state of the existing stock.

The road to sustainable buildings is not a prescribed path and cannot be imposed merely by the application of checklist-based rating systems. Each project has to be considered for its own opportunities and limitations.

Refurbishment projects, while generally being inherently more environmentally desirable because of the raw materials and energy 'embedded' within the buildings, must give due consideration to the sustainability agenda. The integration of innovative features, materials or systems can dramatically improve the environmental performance of an existing building. Operational targets that focus on improved lighting, selection of finishes and materials, comfort conditions, better control and reductions in the energy use of the building will be necessary.

RECOGNISING SUSTAINABILITY IN PRACTICE

Sustainability is always project-specific, meaning that there is no magical checklist that ensures a development will be sustainable in every sense of the word. BREEAM, LEED and similar schemes are useful tools for design teams, but they are only part of the toolbox. The road to sustainable buildings is not a prescribed path and cannot be imposed merely by the application of checklist-based rating systems. Each project has to be considered for its own opportunities and limitations – thus a good sustainable design process should never be mechanised and the importance of 'project-specific thinking' should never be underestimated.

However, it is crucial that developers, occupiers and investors have the requisite tools and understanding to be able to differentiate between the marketing-led 'greenwash' and the truly valuable sustainability features of a building.

Tools for assessing sustainability

For buildings, various rating systems, self-certification schemes and government mandates have been developed in the last two decades and are discussed in detail in Section 4 of this Guide (some already mentioned above).

Although assessment systems address important aspects of sustainability, by their very nature they simplify complex systems into an easily understandable rating. So, does that mean that a highly rated building is 'sustainable'? The answer is: 'It depends...'

Whichever assessment system is used, there are four core principles that should underpin any project that is aiming to achieve a degree of sustainability, which are discussed in more detail throughout this Guide, but which are worth reiterating here, by way of a summary:

→ **Minimise energy consumption.** This all-encompassing principle should be the significant driver during the design process; Considering choice of site (where possible to reduce car-based commuting), orientation of the building (to improve daylighting and passive heating/cooling/ventilation opportunities), design concept, materials, building services, and so on.

→ **Minimise 'embodied energy'.** Materials production and transportation is responsible for a significant proportion of the sectors' environmental impact, so the selection and specification of materials is an important factor in an office building. As the carbon emissions associated with the operation of buildings falls, the significance of the carbon emissions associated with producing building materials and components becomes more important, so design teams should make decisions based on a balance between whole-life cost and environmental impact. Materials should have the lowest possible embodied energy, and be from sustainable sources, and in part be made up of recycled materials (the government-backed agency, WRAP recommends a minimum target of 10% recycled building content by value).

→ **Minimise waste.** The management of waste during construction starts during design, with thought being directed at ways of reducing waste and managing or reusing any demolition resources. The recently introduced Site Waste Management Plans provide a mandatory framework for improving waste management during construction.

→ **Think local.** From reducing transport of materials to choosing local contractors and craftsmen, this aim can dramatically improve a building's sustainability credential – particular so when design factors are also taken into consideration. Office design for a more sustainable building needs to work within the local microclimate. Solutions for an office in a city centre can be very different from an out-of-town greenfield site. Rainfall, sunshine hours, wind speeds and air temperatures can all change the economic viability of building systems. Sustainability is about fitting in with the local environment and ecological and transport issues must be considered along with the need for the building to use less water and energy. The viability of a wind turbine is far greater in the Scottish highlands than in central London. Rain water harvesting in the Lake District will collect more water than one in East Anglia. A solar thermal hot water collector in Cornwall has the ability to generate more energy than one in Cumbria. Location matters, and a sustainable office will work with the opportunities offered by the unique ecological and climate variations of that site.

1.4

WORKING TOGETHER – THE 21ST-CENTURY APPROACH TO BUILDING DESIGN

Integrated design brings the team together to leverage collective knowledge and use a broad range of tools to come up with an optimum solution for a sustainable building project.

So, what will the office buildings of the future look like?
Odds are that they will appear similar to today's buildings, but there will be numerous 'hidden' differences that will deliver the sustainability we desire.

Already, many teams who have adopted the integrated approach to design are developing designs that benefit from thorough site analysis in relation to solar control and building orientation. This basic decision as to how the building is laid out and the extent of glazing in the façade will have a profound impact on the performance – and look – of the building.

More and more buildings are moving away from the floor-to-ceiling clear glass solutions prevalent in office design at the end of the 20th Century, instead incorporating large areas of solid façade or external solar shading, as dictated by the orientation of the building. This greatly reduces the solar thermal impact on the building and makes the use of more passive ventilation solutions viable. This more dynamic approach to achieving comfort levels will become more the norm as design teams strive to meet ever increasing sustainability targets to mitigate climate change.

3 HARDMAN STREET, MANCHESTER
Copyright: Hufton + Crowe

Internally, the changing style of use by occupiers who, in their goal of obtaining more value from their space, will drive forward the more flexible design of cores – to allow levels of occupation to change over a period of time.

The strategy for increasing levels of occupation needs to be understood at the outset, with a densification strategy agreed at the detail design stage. It will then be down to the designers and engineers to devise cores that can flex by allowing additional WCs and risers to be added, without the need for extensive works to the building.

Globalisation is affecting organisations, availability of finance, construction materials and development standards. Office developments will increasingly be expected to reflect international expectations of urbanisation.

Five factors are likely to make the transition to a non-fossil-fuel world far more difficult than is commonly realised:
→ The scale of shift
→ The lower energy density of such fuels
→ The lower power density of renewable energy extraction
→ The intermittency of renewable energy resources
→ The uneven distribution of renewable resources.

All conspire to make the highly desirable non-fossil-fuel world reliant on great determination, cost and many decades of development and implementation.

There will need to be a continuous and sometimes radical change in the approach to the design, construction and operation of buildings, not just in the office sector, if substantial reductions in carbon emissions are to be achieved.

30 ST MARY AXE, SWISS RE HEADQUARTERS
Copyright: Foster + Partners. Photographer: Nigel Young

2.0 /

SITE ISSUES

What to build and where to build it are fundamental questions that all clients need to address. Developing a 'strategic brief' at the outset of a project is a tried-and-tested way to answer these questions and to ensure that the project delivers the intended outcome.

TALKING POINTS

Sustainability

Business performance

Cost & value

2.0 /

2.1

The method of funding or acquisition of the development will impact on the valuation of available tax relief. Land may have to be valued in support of a subsequent claim.

STRATEGIC BRIEF

It is important for the client to develop a strategic brief at the outset of the project. This will enable the design team to focus on the delivery of the design, while assessing the achievability of all aspects of the brief. The review should identify the following:

→ Target market
→ Viability
→ Capital expenditure
→ Construction cost and cashflow
→ Architectural aspirations
→ Target area

→ Efficiency
→ Development programme
→ Engineering systems
→ Sustainability targets
→ Cost in use
→ Performance criteria
→ Quality.

It is also important to set targets and review each target at the concept stage of the design. Decisions taken at this early part of the process will fix the majority of the final design and hence the built solution.

301/302 BRIDGEWATER PLACE, BIRCHWOOD PARK, WARRINGTON
Photographer: Martin Hamilton Knight

MOOR HOUSE, LONDON
Photographer: Will Pryce

2.2

LOCATION

The diagram below highlights the key differences between urban and non-urban locations; and Section 3 highlights the differences between the two options in terms of the building form. However, both developers and end-users view the following points as key to the selection of development sites and the occupation of buildings:

→ The ability to build efficient, usable floor plates to a density that makes the overall development viable
→ The presence of convenient transport facilities or sufficient car park provision
→ The proximity of a new or existing workforce that will allow occupiers to meet their resource requirements
→ The availability of local amenities and support facilities
→ Good quality external environment and adjacent tenants/occupiers
→ The overall impact of the above drivers on sustainability and the ability to retain staff.

Urban	Non-urban
→ Availability of public transport	→ Reliance on car
→ More transport options	→ Fewer transport options
→ Proximity to dedicated cycle routes	→ More car parking
→ Less car parking	→ Lower operational costs
→ Higher operational costs	→ Higher energy and pollution costs (when transport taken into account)
→ Lower energy and pollution costs	→ Lower construction cost
→ Higher construction costs	→ Lower land value
→ Higher land value	

2.3

DENSITY

Development density – expressed as the ratio of gross external building footprint area to site area (plot ratio) – must strike a balance between value, amenity and quality of design.

For non-urban business park developments, plot ratios of 50% are common, providing efficient, regular floor plates in good quality environments.

CHISWICK PARK
Courtesy of Stanhope Copyright: Hufton + Crowe

Urban sites generally offer very high plot ratios when compared with non-urban locations. Although urban developments do not have the same potential to benefit from less-energy-intensive servicing solutions such as natural ventilation as the lower density shallow plan non-urban sites, they can still provide sustainable development, given the reduction in transport-generated carbon emissions provided by public transport links.

Urban developments will potentially have less regular floor plates, given local constraints, and have a higher build cost. Groupings of small buildings result in lower optimum densities than the provision of larger buildings of a similar total area because more space is required for road access to small buildings and because smaller footplates are usually less space efficient. Buildings with larger footplates are also more cost-effective to build and operate due to the lower wall to floor ratio.

■■■

2.4

Land Remediation Relief allows a developer to recover up to 14% of its costs in the year of sale. An investor can claim up to 42% of its costs.

■■■

SITE ANALYSIS

Offices, whether located on business parks or in urban areas, share many common key characteristics in terms of the analysis required to truly understand the site.

Site analysis should consider:
→ Adaptive re-use of existing buildings
→ Orientation and topography
→ Light from the sky – hours and angle
→ Wind direction and frequency for prevailing winds.
→ Degree of exposure
→ Day and night temperatures
→ Types and locations of trees and shrubs providing wind shelter
→ Local obstructions that may affect the availability of light and solar radiation to the building
→ Views worth preserving
→ Water table and tidal patterns
→ Local wildlife patterns, wildlife corridors, and biodiversity
→ The patterns of any existing pedestrian, bicycle and vehicular movement across and around the site
→ The availability of public transport
→ Road congestion
→ Urban air pollution and noise levels on site
→ Local potential for the use of renewable energy sources
→ Opportunity for on-site waste recycling/digestion
→ Remediation strategies for brownfield sites.

Although there will be many influences from the surrounding context or from pre-agreed masterplans, early site analysis should review the following:

→ **Building orientation:** This will have a significant impact on internal conditions and the potential to utilise more passive environmental systems. The relationship between the orientation and façade/solar control design will affect the amount of sunlight incident on the building and heat gain within the building. The correct decisions made at this stage will have a large impact on the carbon emissions of the building throughout its life (see Figure 2.1).

→ **Environmental systems:** The potential for more passive systems should be thoroughly considered on all sites (using, for example, simulation software).

→ **Local potential for renewables on site:** Solar, wind and water should all be considered with a view to maximising renewables on site.

Figure 2.1 Solar control stategies

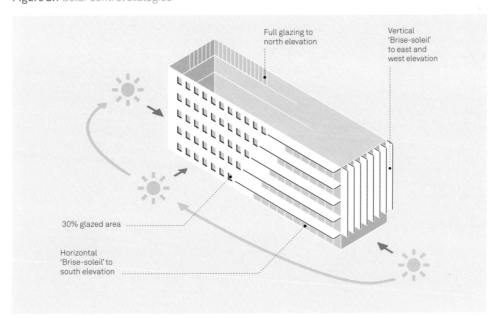

Full glazing to north elevation

Vertical 'Brise-soleil' to east and west elevation

30% glazed area

Horizontal 'Brise-soleil' to south elevation

2.4.1

£ £ Where grant funding
or third-party subsidies
are received, available capital
allowances may be diluted.
Proper planning can help to
avoid this.

CONSTRAINTS

It is important to establish the following basic levels of
information relating to the site:

→ The regional impacts of the proposed development on the
watershed, flooding, wetlands, wildlife habits and
transportation
→ The environmental opportunities of the site (identified by the
study of the microclimate, geology, hydrology, and ecology of
the site, and documented in the site analysis drawings).

Detailed site analysis should be carried out to ensure that the
impact of the building on the local environment is minimised, and
that the potential for utilising natural resources is maximised.

Features such as railways and roads, which may adversely
affect the quality of the space, should also be considered,
and could be controlled by the quality and performance of
the external envelope.

The orientation of the building can have a significant impact
on the potential to maximise passive design and reduce the
building's environmental impact. In some cases, such as in
constricted city centre sites or due to access road restrictions,
orientation choices can be limited. In these circumstances
exploiting passive strategies is more challenging, but it is not
impossible. The issues remain the same as stated overleaf,
but there will be a trade-off in terms of what can be achieved.

FURTHER READING
*Environmental Design
Guide for Naturally
Ventilated and Daylit
Offices*, BRE

The aspects of design that are affected by orientation and the site include:

→ Maximising the capacity for natural daylighting and the average daylight factor while minimising glare (for example, by incorporating sunlight solar shading devices including light shelves to extend the light deeper into the floor-plate across the office)
→ Reducing the potential for overheating by screening and shading the façades
→ Maximising the potential for passive cooling
→ Exploiting the opportunity for renewable technologies
→ Maximise capture of solar energy
→ Enhancing comfort in outdoor spaces (both in terms of personal safety, and from a design point of view by, for instance, not creating wind tunnels)
→ Creating and using vegetation heat sinks
→ Zoning internal spaces to provide buffers to suit the requirements for natural daylighting, heating, cooling and ventilation.

ICON BUSINESS CENTRES, 1400 PARK APPROACH, LEEDS

2.5

 External spaces can affect the buildings that define them, particularly in an urban environment where pleasant public spaces can be few and far between. The design of these spaces should consider solar shading, wind shelter, pollution dispersal and spacing to ensure that sunlight can reach both the space itself and the surrounding buildings.

PUBLIC REALM

Site analysis will inform the most appropriate way to integrate the building within the public realm.

The design of the space, using soft and hard materials in combination with water features and public art, will make a significant contribution to the quality of the local environment.

The landscape design should:
→ Enhance the architecture of the building and be integrated into its overall design
→ Provide amenity space for any alternative uses, such as retail and residential components of the overall masterplan
→ Emphasise the way-finding around the site and assist in marking out the building entrance
→ Provide shelter from wind and sun, so that external space can be enjoyed for longer periods of the year
→ Be fully integrated into the overall environmental response to the building via, for example, the provision of external shading, free water cooling and rainwater harvesting
→ Improve the security of the site and the safety of individuals in the public environment. (See Appendix A1: Safety, security and risk.)

NEW STREET SQUARE
Copyright: The Liquid Way

1 KINGDOM STREET
Photograph: Smoothe

2.6

£ £ Mixed-use schemes
will impact on the use
and nature of eligible plant
assets. Decorative assets can
be considered as qualifying
in hotel and restaurant
settings. Plant and machinery
assets in residential areas do
not qualify. Additionally,
differential VAT rates may
be considered for residential
elements.

MIXED USE

The 2005 edition of the BCO Guide *Best practice in the
specification of offices* identified five key drivers of mixed use
development: fad or fashion; policy; social; economic; and
technical. But times have changed, and so have the drivers,
which are currently as follows:

→ **Planning policy** – remains a key driver of mixed use
development, although policy varies from one planning
authority to the next. Some local authority policies require
residential space when increased commercial density is
created (usually when density increase exceeds a defined
threshold). Debate continues over whether mixed use is
appropriate for every site versus intensity of use being the
greatest influence on the creation of urban communities.
Where mixed use is appropriate, it is important that use mix
is considered carefully in order to create a development where
each of the uses complements the others, and that the end
development gains the inherent benefit of such things as
safety by design, extension of trading hours, provision of
amenity for commercial occupiers and residential occupiers
etc. Dependant on market conditions a mix of uses can
improve development viability.

One of the strongest commercial
influences on the mixed use
agenda is the perceived flexibility
during and after planning
determination, adjusting uses
to suit market conditions.

→ **The principal use** – This is dictated by
circumstance of location and economics.
Deciding which element is the 'principal use'
often involves reaching an acceptable
compromise. In mixed use buildings it is
almost inevitable that one or other of the
use types will have a dominant effect on the
structural solution chosen. The concept of
the principal use is, of course, more difficult
to apply to a project which may have more
than one developer.

→ **Economics** – In recent years, land acquisition costs have been significantly influenced by the effects of mixed use policy. Construction cost and investment value in vertical mixed-use projects is generally less sensitive because there is independent consideration of each use. Whereas a horizontal use mix has higher risk of cost uncertainty and, more importantly, how costs are attributed either during phasing or in additional costs as a result of structural or services on cost attribution. Consideration also needs to be given to the impact on whole life costs of refurbishment and redevelopment in horizontally layered mixed use developments, where tenure differs and operational activities can be difficult to manage.

→ **Flexibility** – One of the strongest commercial influences on the mixed use agenda is the perceived flexibility during and after planning determination, adjusting uses to suit market conditions. On mixed use sites where use is defined by plot, i.e. where uses are separated vertically, this can be a relatively easy proposition. Whereas if a mix of uses is contained within one volume (normally divided horizontally), the longer term flexibility is only possible by careful choice of structural grid, service strategy and the location and possible sharing of cores.

→ **Ownership** – On mixed use sites with clear separation of building plots the issue of ownership is clear and careful infrastructure planning can allow for independence of tenure and ownership. The particular sensitivities of residential adjacencies (and affordable provision) are becoming increasingly common, and as a result, there are precedents for the resolution of layout and practical sharing of infrastructure.

→ **Management** – Single point management can be beneficial for the long-term success of any mixed scheme, and of critical importance in high density mixed-use buildings. The equitable sharing of management costs is always a difficult issue but increasingly solvable by precedent. Of particular note are the following issues: servicing/delivery timing; services (combined heat and power, for example); maintenance and access; car parking; amenity versus commerciality; corporate and private territory; infrastructure; interface with local community; interface with public services (refuse, fire etc).

2.0 / SITE ISSUES

BISHOPS SQUARE, LONDON
Copyright: Hammerson

2.6.1

SUSTAINABILITY AND MIXED USE

Mixed used developments present opportunities for enhancing sustainability in terms of benefiting the environment, creating a community, and improving energy efficiency.

In the broadest sense, the environmental benefits of reduced journey times, higher density allowing for proper public transport provision, reducing the number of journeys made by private transport and so on are all laudable. However, the reality of our continued dependence on private transport and the strength of this as a driver is an irony which needs to be honestly addressed.

The scale of a development may be such that it can create a self-sufficient and evolving 'district'.

The possibility of providing a sustainable community is a complex issue, which should be considered very carefully. The scale of a development may be such that it can create its own self-sufficient (in some ways) and evolving 'district', which is clearly beneficial. Careful judgement must be exercised about how this may integrate into the broader community in which the development fits. The consideration of this is more about the intensity of use rather than the density of development.

In theory, a more complex mix of uses allows for greater efficiencies in energy consumption – waste heat from retail or commercial being used to heat domestic water, or the use of a combined heat and power (CHP) system being obvious examples. In practice, larger schemes take longer to build and few developers are prepared to have complete CHP provision in the first phases of a project. The opportunities for both heat exchange and CHP use depend on the scale and nature of the development, and the mix and the prospect of phasing.

APPROACHES TO MIXED USE

There are several ways of approaching mixed use, and the choice is generally informed by the size of the site.

BANKSIDE, LONDON
Photographer: Paul Grundy

For large sites (where the plot exceeds the size of a single building) a master-planning approach should be adopted. The mix of uses will be informed by planning policy, market demand for the individual uses, density and financial viability (as described above). Although it is not always the case, large plots – where a number of individual buildings are deliverable – offer the opportunity for uses to be separated by building, for example, separate buildings for office, residential, hotel, retail, student housing and so on. This gives the advantages of clarity of sub-division, ease of phasing, structural clarity/ efficiency, the potential for simple partnering arrangements, and it avoids the challenges of tenure where residential space forms part of a single mixed use building.

For smaller sites, typically where a single building is the appropriate option, the mix of uses will need to be contained in a single envelope. The options are to divide the uses horizontally or vertically and much is dependant on plot size, building shape and the level of density that is required. This type of approach is generally (though not universally) found in highly dense urban environments and where planning policy or financial viability push the developer towards such a solution.

FURTHER READING
The technical
aspects of mixed-use
developments are
discussed in Appendix
A4: Mixed use:
Technical issues

Challenges include potentially higher structural and building
engineering services costs, lower building net to gross
efficiencies and careful consideration of residential tenure.

Table 2.1 compares these options:

Table 2.1 Advantages and disadvantages of mixed use types

Masterplan-driven; separate plots	
Advantages	**Disadvantages**
→ Clarity of sub-division	→ Lower density sites only
→ Ease of phasing	→ Front-loading of infrastructure costs
→ Structural clarity	
→ Simple partnering arrangements	

High density; horizontal divisions	
Advantages	**Disadvantages**
→ Maximising site value (subject to minimising build cost)	→ Potentially higher structural costs
→ Energy sharing options	→ Usually higher costs for services, especially electrical provision
→ Careful phasing allows for flexibility of use allocation and can adapt to market conditions	→ Less straightforward to joint venture (allocation of infrastructure/structural costs)
→ Generally finds favour with planning authorities	→ Often requires a very high density to fund the complexity which may not be permitted by planning
→ Makes for better cities	→ More complex management requirements
	→ Refurbishment, redevelopment and plant replacement more difficult
	→ High density; vertical division
	→ Tenure may restrict future flexibility

High density; vertical division	
Advantages	**Disadvantages**
→ Easier to phase and share funding	→ Few sites offer the luxury of sub-division
→ Greater structural flexibility	
→ Faster construction	
→ Greater flexibility	

61

2.0 /

2.7

RE-USE OF EXISTING BUILDINGS

The demolition and redevelopment of a building involves the removal of thousands of tonnes of construction material and the procurement, delivery and assembly of thousands of tonnes of new material. Energy used in the construction of a building currently accounts for approximately 15% of the total carbon emissions that can be attributed to the building over its lifecycle (i.e. its carbon footprint, discussed in Section 4: Sustainability). As operational energy performance improves over the next 10–15 years, the environmental cost of site clearance and construction may rise to 30% of the total.

Given that approximately 90% of UK office space is in buildings that are more than ten years old, meaningful reductions in the overall environmental impact of office buildings can only be achieved by the widespread re-use of existing building stock.

Improvements to the environmental performance of existing buildings will have a very significant effect on the overall environmental performance of the office sector. By contrast, initiatives aimed at improving the performance of new buildings will affect only the small amount of new space that is developed (currently in the order of 1% per year).

40 EASTBOURNE TERRACE
BEFORE REFURBISHMENT
Photographer: Chris Gascoigne

40 EASTBOURNE TERRACE
AFTER REFURBISHMENT
Photographer: Chris Gascoigne

2.7.1	IDENTIFYING VALUE

There is a growing awareness of the potential value in existing fabric and infrastructure, and creative adaptation instead of demolition and redevelopment has delivered some remarkable buildings.

Office buildings have traditionally been seen as either new-build or second-hand/refurbished, with negative market perceptions of second-hand stock. As occupiers become more concerned with environmental matters, the perceived stigma of second-hand buildings may turn out to be a positive factor: if a building can be shown to work well in terms of business performance and operational efficiency, the fact that it has been brought into being with a minimum of embodied energy should count as a further point in its favour.

If the building form is capable of satisfying some (though not all) best practice criteria and if it is capable of accommodating appropriate engineering solutions, then refurbishment or adaptation can deliver tangible benefits.

There is a growing incidence of refurbishment and recycling in speculative development, as more developers recognise this approach as a route to profit through:

→ Capital cost savings by re-use of existing fabric
→ Time saving and reduction of risk due to simplified planning and construction processes
→ Reduced environmental impact by the avoidance of demolition and replacement.

When the envelope of an existing building is performing poorly and its services have reached the end of their useful life, it may be perceived as having little remaining value. However, it may still be capable of adaptation to meet the highest contemporary standards as indeed is the case for buildings that are located in conservation areas or are subject to statutory listing.

2.7.2

DESIGN OPTIONS

The underlying intention will be to achieve performance comparable with a new building, at a lower cost in both financial and environmental terms. As such, the best practice guidelines set out elsewhere in this guide should be followed where possible. However, each case must be viewed on its merit. As an example, many refurbishments have produced excellent office space with floor-to-ceiling dimensions of less than the recommended clear heights for new build given in Section 3.1.

 A key factor in determining the appropriate degree of intervention will be the relative performance of different elements of the existing building, and the extent to which they have reached the end of their useful life. Opportunities arise when one or more elements can be seen to be underperforming. Consideration should be given to:

→ **Structure**
- rationalising/improving plan form
- selecting a fit-out strategy to reveal thermal mass
- allowing space for additional mechanical and electrical (M&E) services to support a potential increase in the density of occupants.

→ **Envelope**
- insulation
- air tightness
- solar shading
- natural ventilation
- passive cooling capability
- solar heating/photovoltaics.

→ **Services**
- incorporating passive techniques where possible
- designing active systems for long life and low energy consumption
- avoiding over-specification but incorporating an upgrade path to support a potential increase in the density of occupants.

2.7.3

Repairs are fully
deductible for tax
although restrictions exist
where integral features
are repaired. Where new
plant assets are installed,
incidental structural works
may qualify for relief.

REFURBISHMENT STRATEGIES

Many of the perceived shortcomings of older buildings, including limited servicing options and restricted floor-to-floor heights, can now be overcome through advances in environmental and communications technology.

In order to establish the potential of an existing building to support a 'new' lifecycle, it is important to:

→ Analyse plan dimensions against BCO best practice criteria
→ Analyse section dimensions in terms of ceiling height and servicing requirements (reductions below the standard floor to ceiling height recommended in this document, have proven to be acceptable in occupation)
→ Evaluate options for upgrading envelope performance
→ Develop servicing strategy to achieve excellent working conditions and operational efficiency.

All elements will naturally be subject to cost/benefit analysis. In the context of changing perceptions and legislation, the criteria for evaluating benefits are in a constant state of flux; higher aspirations for operational energy efficiency are shortening both the effective lifecycle of poorly performing components and the payback period for their replacement. The calculation may include, in addition to conventional financial criteria, a comparative evaluation of embodied energy cost for refurbishment against demolition/redevelopment to achieve a given end result.

2.7.4

 Asbestos stripped out of existing buildings may be eligible for 150% Land Remediation Relief.

 Consider whether the building is listed or in a disadvantaged area. Business Premises Renovation Allowance may be available with up to 100% of the cost being available for tax relief.

FURTHER RECYCLING OPTIONS

If analysis shows that a building does not lend itself to profitable refurbishment, there may still be valid 'recycling' solutions, including a programme of extension or new construction that incorporates significant aspects of the substructure, structure or envelope elements of the existing buildings on the site.

For example, where not only the envelope but even the cores are shown to be unsuitable for re-use, the refurbishment strategy may extend to stripping the building back to its structural frame, supplementing the core accommodation as part of a more radical transformation. This begins to move beyond refurbishment to a more radical re-use of the existing structure. Even if none of the structure above ground is retained, re-use of basements or just existing piles can be considered.

Although the driver for refurbishment is often the dwindling asset value of an obsolete office building, there are many examples of industrial or other buildings in locations once regarded as unsuitable for offices which are now becoming too valuable for their previous use. Where a building was built for non-office use, the dimensions of its structural grid may nevertheless offer a good match for best practice office criteria. Even if the existing building's overall plan footprint and storey heights may be unsuitable, the ground floor slab, substructure, drainage and site infrastructure may be capable of supporting an entirely new purpose-designed superstructure. Significant savings, both financial and environmental, may be achieved from these elements alone.

The refurbishment strategy may extend to stripping the building back to its structural frame

55 BAKER STREET, LONDON
Photographer: Will Pryce

3.0 /

BUILDIN
FORM

Form follows function. Design parameters are the foundation to any design. They vary for building type and location and are considered here.

G

TALKING
POINTS

Sustainability

Business
performance

Cost & value

3.0 /

BUILDING FORM

3.1

SPACE CONFIGURATION

3.1.1

DEEP PLAN BUILDING

Window to window, or atrium: 15–21 m
This provides large, flexible floor plates. However, the increased
depth will require mechanical environmental controls to maintain
internal conditions.

Window to core: 6–12 m
(In some circumstances deeper zones can work.)

Finished floor to underside of ceiling: 2.6–2.75 m
For some time this has been a standard for general office space,
but it is commonly raised to 3.0 m for deeper office space (i.e.
over 18 m and greater for specialist areas such as trading floors).

Key considerations for deep plan buildings:
→ Higher capital costs
→ Higher running costs
→ Flexible, efficient space
→ Ability to occupy space densely while maintaining consistent
   internal conditions.

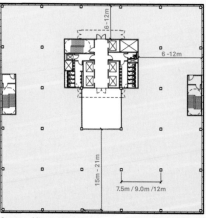

Courtesy of Sheppard Robson

3.1.2

SHALLOW PLAN BUILDING

Window to window, or atrium: 12.0–15.0 m
This will allow the potential use of natural ventilation, but will need to be carefully integrated with the external envelope to allow its controlled use.

Window to core: 6.0–7.5 m

Finished floor to underside of ceiling: 2.6–3.0 m
This range allows for maximising daylight penetration and reducing the need for artificial light. The necessity of suspended ceilings should be challenged, given the passive cooling benefit obtained from the thermal mass of an exposed structure.

Key considerations for shallow plan buildings:
→ Lower capital cost (if non-air-conditioned)
→ Lower running costs (if non-air-conditioned)
→ Potential occupant control via opening windows
→ Two zone planning will affect occupation flexibility at 12 m depths
→ Higher levels of temperature differential over the year (if non-air-conditioned).

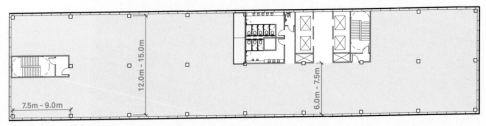

Courtesy of Sheppard Robson

BBC SCOTLAND HEADQUARTERS, PACIFIC QUAY, GLASGOW
Photographer: Michael Boyd

3.1.3

ATRIA AND INTERNAL STREETS

The use of atria in conjunction with deep plan office floor plates can improve unit costs by optimising the useful floor area created for a given volume enclosed by the envelope, and will introduce natural light. This can also reduce running costs by providing a climatic buffer zone between internal environmentally controlled space and the external environment.

Employing building shapes based on atria can improve plate efficiency and increase creative space planning options. Atria provide the opportunity to create a social hub for occupant interaction.

Enclosed atria solutions are usually driven by the need to provide multi-occupier segregation, fire regulations, space comfort control and acoustic issues.

Open atria solutions are more acceptable to single organisation occupiers, when they can be used to assist the operation of mixed mode and natural ventilation solutions in shallow plan, low rise buildings.

In larger buildings, atria should ideally be designed to enable infill at any point in the future should more floor area be required due to a change in user workspace requirements, or a need to create deeper plan space (for example, to accommodate a dealer area).

SONY COMPUTER ENTERTAINMENT, LONDON
Copyright: Morey Smith

3.0 /

3.2

Net Internal Area (NIA):
The lettable area
within a building
measured at 1.5 m
above finished floor
level to the internal
face of the perimeter
walls of each floor
level excluding core
elements, plant rooms
and columns.

Gross Internal Area
(GIA): The whole
building measured to
the inside face of the
external walls.

Gross External Area
(GEA): The whole
building measured to
the outside face of the
external walls.

FURTHER READING
*Code of Measuring
Practice*, RICS Books

*BCO Occupier Density
Study*, 2009

OCCUPANCY STANDARDS

Occupiers wanting to maximise their use of space are increasingly considering two measures of density. The most robust measure for occupation density is 'workplace density':

→ Workplace density is the net internal area (NIA) divided by the number of workspaces.
→ Effective density is NIA divided by maximum occupancy.

Workplace density: 8–13 m^2 per workplace

During the period May–August 2008, the BCO commissioned research into the current occupancy density of commercial offices in the UK. The study covered 249 UK properties, constituting over 2,000,000 m^2 of net internal area in a variety of tenancy arrangements for a wide range of business occupiers.

The distribution of the sample results from the study (shown in Figure 3.1, opposite) indicate that 77% of the sampled properties have an occupation density of between 8 m^2 and 13 m^2 per workspace NIA.

The study revealed that office space is being more intensively planned, occupied and managed. This is a response to changing work patterns, which require more imaginative space planning solutions, greater use of open plan rather than cellular offices, reduced desk sizes, desk sharing and remote working.

Figure 3.1 BCO's 2008 occupancy density survey

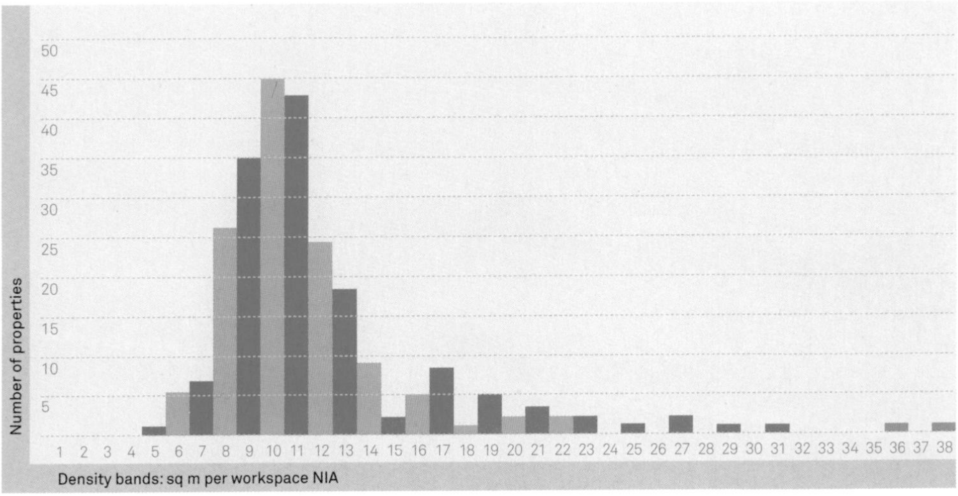

To date, there is little evidence that building infrastructure designed in accordance with previous BCO guidance is failing to accommodate these higher workplace densities. This is partly explained by the fact that utilisation rates are typically well below 100%, and thus effective density is lower than workplace density. This situation may change, as occupiers seek greater efficiency from their property resource and in response to this, the guidance given in this edition of the guide has been revised.

The study also revealed that the maximum utilisation of workplaces in many organisations is in the range of 50–60% with the highest recorded at around 80%.

It is important to note that considering workplace density alone may overstate the demands placed on building infrastructure, or result in over provision if used as the basis for design. The effect of applying utilisation rates is shown in Table 3.1. Effective density, expressed as NIA per person, is a better guide to actual demands on building infrastructure.

Table 3.1 Effective density (sq m NIA per person)

		Utilisation									
		100%	95%	90%	85%	80%	75%	70%	65%	60%	55%	50%
Workplace density (m²)	7	7.0	7.4	7.8	8.2	8.8	9.3	10.0	10.8	11.7	12.7	14.0
	8	8.0	8.4	8.9	9.4	10.0	10.7	11.4	12.3	13.3	14.5	16.0
	9	9.0	9.5	10.0	10.6	11.3	12.0	12.9	13.8	15.0	16.4	18.0
	10	10.0	10.5	11.1	11.8	12.5	13.3	14.3	15.4	16.7	18.2	20.0
	11	11.0	11.6	12.2	12.9	13.8	14.7	15.7	16.9	18.3	20.0	22.0
	12	12.0	12.6	13.3	14.1	15.0	16.0	17.1	18.5	20.0	21.8	24.0
	13	13.0	13.7	14.4	15.3	16.2	17.3	18.6	20.0	21.7	23.6	26.0

For developments where the actual workplace density and maximum utilisation are not known, it is necessary to adopt best practice design guidelines which reflect a reasonable balance between the initial provision made by the developer and enhancements carried out by an occupier to suit their particular specific requirements, which will vary across and between floors. These design parameters also need to recognise the relationship.

Workplace density: 10 m² per workspace NIA
Use this value for services design, air conditioning loads, outdoor air allowances and small power loads, and so on.

Effective density: 12 m² per person NIA
Use this value for core design elements, WC provision, lift capacity, and so on.

See also, Appendix A2:
Statutory regulations

Means of escape density: 6 m² per person NIA
This value is based on maximum allowable floor occupation
density as defined in the Building Regulations Document
Part B. This criterion can be relaxed, by agreement with
Building Control, on the understanding that if building occupation
density increases in the future, modifications would have to be
made to the building staircases and means of escape provisions.
Good practice would suggest that relaxations greater than
8 m² per person are unduly restrictive and would significantly
reduce the flexibility of the building to accommodate a range
of occupiers needs.

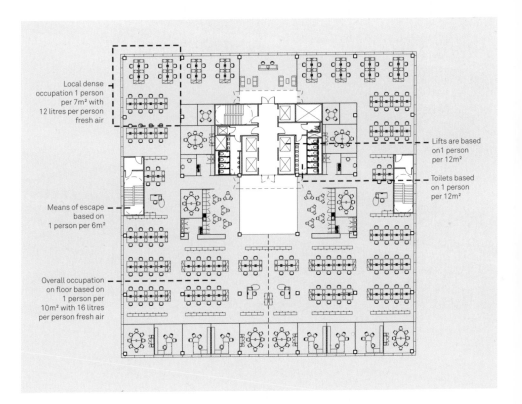

Local dense
occupation 1 person
per 7m² with
12 litres per person
fresh air

Lifts are based
on 1 person
per 12m²

Toilets based
on 1 person
per 12m²

Means of escape
based on
1 person per 6m²

Overall occupation
on floor based on
1 person per
10m² with 16 litres
per person fresh air

8, FITZROY STREET, LONDON
Copyright: Arup/Hufton + Crowe

3.3

Cores are frequently used as important structural elements to stabilise the building and as such may be constructed as reinforced concrete walls or braced steel frames. Their design requires the careful co-ordination of potentially conflicting requirements, namely; the integrity of structural load paths and the provision of routes for the distribution of people and services.

CORE ELEMENTS

A key driver in the efficiency and flexibility of the building is the design of the core. The main core contains the operational components of the building that provide vertical circulation, escape stairs, WCs and the main distribution for mechanical, electrical and plumbing services.

Large buildings may have more than one main core, allowing separate entrances and enhancing building flexibility. If this is the case, the main core will be supported by secondary escape cores, the number dependant on floor plate size and means of escape requirements. The secondary core or cores contain alternative means of escape stairs and, often, vertical service distribution risers and amenity facilities.

The distance between the principal and secondary core should be maximised to allow them to serve the largest floor area possible.

The key factors for determining the location of the main core are as follows:
→ Its location on the floor plate should seek to maximise the efficiency and usefulness of the floor plate.
→ Its relationship to the ground floor reception should aim to reduce extensive travel distances from the reception to the lifts.
→ The location should allow the floor plate to be subdivided into smaller lettable units with the minimum of circulation space. The use and access to WCs, means of escape and tenants riser space needs to be carefully considered in this exercise. Most flexibility is provided by accessing these facilities from the landlord's areas, as opposed to the office space. However, some occupiers prefer direct access from their demise.

3.3.1

STAIRS

◐◐ Staircases should
be located for building
users to have the option to use
them instead of lifts, with the
design of the staircases providing
visual connection and social
interaction opportunities. Energy
consumption associated with lifts
(in terms of embodied energy and
energy in use) is high, so encourage
the use of staircases to help in the
carbon reduction strategy.

Escape and accommodation stairs should be designed to:
→ Meet the maximum envisaged occupancy density on the floors.
  (Building Regulations guidance recommends 1 person per 6 m^2
  but this can be relaxed, subject to specific agreement with the
  Building Control Authority)
→ Be located and made easily identifiable to encourage use for
  inter-floor circulation.

3.3.2

LIFTS

Lifts and lift lobbies are a key element in the design and
efficiency of the core, occupying a significant area. The use
of lifts to ensure the efficient movement of people and goods
through a building, particularly tall buildings, is critical to
achieving a productive workplace.

The performance of the passenger lifts is
defined in terms of quantity, how effective they
are in moving the building population into the
building, quality of performance and waiting
times. Section 7 provides detailed guidance
on the selection and performance of lifts
and escalators.

Lifts also play an important role in times of
emergency, providing evacuation facilities for
disabled people and secure access for fire
fighting personnel within a protected area
of the principal and or secondary core areas.

1 KINGDOM STREET
Photographer: SectorLight

3.3.3

WASHROOMS

The requirement for toilet provision is based on the occupancy of the space and therefore is defined by the overall net floor area and the anticipated density of occupation. The relevant UK standard is BS 6465. This Standard is currently under review, but is likely to call for occupancy to be calculated on 1 person per 10 m^2, based on a male:female split of 60%:60%.

Not withstanding this, BCO research suggests that toilet provision should be calculated on the basis of:

Occupation density of 1 per 12 m^2

Male:female ratio: 60%:60% (i.e. 20% excess provision against calculated occupancy)
This reflects a workplace density of 1 person per 10 m^2 with a utilisation factor of 80%.

Unisex applications: 100% provision of floor occupancy (i.e. no excess provision)

Washrooms should be designed to allow ease of extension at the principal core and/or the provision of satellite facilities.

38 FINSBURY SQUARE, LONDON
Copyright: Will Pryce

3.0 /

BUILDING FORM

Tables 3.2 and 3.3 set out the number of fittings required for each sex, once the occupancy level is defined.

Where unisex WCs are used, no excess provision is required and the occupancy is based on 100%. However, as these facilities are generally used for longer periods than shared facilities the new British Standard calls for the number of cubicles to be increased by 25%. These self-contained units provide WC and handwashing facilities, but obviously not urinal facilities (which are still seen as the most efficient way of dealing with male requirements).

Table 3.2 Sanitary appliances for female staff, and for male staff where urinals are not installed

Number of persons at work	Number of WCs	Number of washbasins
1–5	1	1
5–15	2	2
16–30	3	3
31–45	4	4
46–60	5	5
61–75	6	6
76–90	7	7
91–100	8	8
Above 100	8, plus 1 WC and washbasin for every unit or fraction of a unit of 25 persons	

Table 3.3 Alternative scale of provision of sanitary appliances for use by male staff only

Number of persons at work	Number of WCs	Number of urinals	Number of washbasins
1–15	1	1	1
16–30	2	1	2
31–45	2	2	2
46–60	3	2	3
61–75	3	3	3
76–90	4	3	4
91–100	4	4	4
Above 100	4, plus 1 WC urinal and washbasin for every unit or fraction of a unit of 50 males		

FURTHER READING
See also Appendix A3:
Health and Safety

In terms of provisions for disabled people, one cubicle in any group must be accessible by the ambulant disabled (this primarily involves the door being outward opening). Also, if there are four or more cubicles in the group, one must be enlarged to 1200 mm wide, once again to enhance facilities for use by ambulant disabled people. In addition to these requirements a fully wheelchair accessible, unisex WC must be provided per floor.

All requirements should be agreed with the District Surveyor at the start of a project, because some requirements may be omitted (for example, the enlarged cubicle, when the wheelchair accessible cubicle is provided).

The new British Standard when published is expected to confirm that fully accessible disabled WCs can now be included in the overall WC calculations and that calculations must be based on a floor-by-floor basis as opposed to a whole building calculation, which would increase the number of facilities provided.

3.3.4

In order to qualify for a BREEAM credit, showers need to be provided at a ratio of 1 shower per 10 cycle spaces.

SHOWER PROVISION

In recent years, there has been an increase in demand for shower provision in office buildings. This demand has been driven by local planning policy, BREEAM guidance and occupier demand – all responses to changes in the way building users commute to work and often combine fitness and leisure activities within their working day.

Shower facilities can be provided in a central location (by the landlord in multi-let buildings), often in the basement or near to cycle storage areas, or on individual floors in space where washroom facilities are demised to individual occupiers.

FURTHER READING
Workplace (Health,
Safety & Welfare)
Regulations, 1992

The facilities should include changing space, secure lockers, drying space and appropriate privacy for male and female users.

3.3.5

CLEANERS' CUPBOARDS

All office buildings need to make provision for cleaning activities. Storage spaces for toilet supplies are equally important.

The cleaning strategy will influence the quantity and type of cleaning facilities required. Increasingly, modern methods of cleaning rely on environmentally friendly chemical cleaners and micro-fibre dry cloth-based solutions. Where wet cleaning provision is required, cleaners' cupboards containing a Belfast sink and hot and cold running water should be provided.

It is difficult to provide definitive advice on the number and location of cleaners' cupboards and storage facilities, but the following issues should be taken into account when determining the requirements for a specific building:

→ Total building area
→ Individual floor plate size
→ Number of floors
→ Specific cleaning requirements and finishes
→ Core arrangements
→ Washroom location (demised or under landlord control)
→ Cleaning strategy for occupied areas and common parts
  (may negate the need altogether).

3.3.6

DISABLED PROVISION

Where DDA compliance works are incorporated within an existing building, some may be fully tax-deductible as revenue expenditure.

The Disability Discrimination Act (DDA), Building Regulations Approved Document M and BS8300 provide best practice advice on accommodating the needs of disabled people.

It is essential to consider the needs of people with various disabilities, not just wheelchair users. At an early stage this requires due consideration of the following:

→ Access to the building
→ Provision of accessible toilets, including ground floor reception areas
→ Provision of staircases that are accessible to ambulant disabled people
→ Corridor and door widths
→ Wayfinding, manifestation on glass and visual contrast.

FURTHER READING
See also Appendix A3:
Health and Safety

3.4

ENTRANCE AND RECEPTION

The location of the main entrance is primarily determined by the street address and proximity to thoroughfares and to other building entrances.

The reception space provides a series of amenities for the building and needs to serve a number of functions. It is intended to provide a calm, functional and efficient access point to key services for occupiers and visitors, while expressing the brand of the building and, by association, of its occupiers.

The layout and effectiveness of the reception space is crucial to the day-to-day operation of a building, and the choice of interior finishes is an important part of the buildings design. This is the space in an office building that offers one of few opportunities to brand the building and for the occupiers to express their business at the entry point of the building.

133 HOUNDSDITCH, LONDON
Photographer: Will Pryce

The entrance area may include the following:
→ Concierge/reception
→ Security
→ Way finding
→ Security control
→ Waiting /seating area
→ Informal meeting space
→ Interconnection to vertical transportation.

It may be appropriate to include amenity into the reception area, or connection to amenity, such as neighbouring food and coffee facilities, or internet access. Informal meeting space may be appropriate and beneficial to the office space.

The size and volume of the reception depends on a number of factors including the overall size and height of the building, the choice of location of the core and its proximity to the main entrance, and the number of occupants that the entrance will service. Main entrance areas can work equally well as single height or greater and benefit from natural light; they can also interconnect to atria. Generally, in urban environments, activity to ground floor frontages is created by retail and thus the entrance design must consider how the main entrance is able to express itself sufficiently to compete with the power of retail frontages.

Large buildings may have a secondary entrance that allows for executive and staff access, or where it is helpful to provide access from more than one street.

Scalability of the main reception area by incorporating options for inclusion of adjacent retail space (if required by an occupier) should be considered at the design stage.

FURTHER READING
BCO Security Guide
2009
See also Appendix
A1: Safety, Security
and Risk

Building security is generally provided by a combination of security staff and automatic security barriers. The size of the building will influence the need and demand for dedicated reception personnel.

3.5

Sustainable urban drainage should be considered for surface level parking areas.

VEHICULAR ACCESS AND PARKING

Parking levels vary significantly between urban and non-urban locations.

For urban locations, progressive planning policies have reduced parking numbers to minimum levels and in many cases it is now accepted that car parking spaces are not provided. In the same period there has been an increased requirement for cycle and motor cycle parking.

It is usual for any parking provision to be provided underground, accessed from street level by either ramp or car lift. Space for proper servicing of the building and taxi drop off should be considered as part of the building design.

FURTHER READING
BCO Security Guide
2009

See also Appendix
A1: Safety, Security
and Risk

Where urban office space is created as part of a mixed use development, and particularly where residential space is part of the development, parking spaces will be needed.

3.0 /

Parking areas should be designed with security in mind, providing a secure and safe environment for the user

Non-urban environments, which are less well supported by public transport links than urban locations, will have greater requirements for on-site parking than urban locations. Generally, this will be satisfied by surface-level parking, and in an open air environment external to the building envelope. For high density sites consideration may be given to the creation of parking below the office space and within the boundary of the building envelope, often by a cut-and-fill operation to mask the parking areas and to create naturally ventilated parking space, avoiding the need for the complexity of mechanical ventilation.

In all cases, parking areas should be designed with security in mind, providing a secure and safe environment for the user. Pedestrian walkways, good levels of illumination, CCTV and provision for the disabled should be provided. For surface level parking it is usual to enhance the environment with landscaping which should be carefully considered to ensure that the safety of users is not compromised.

Large scale non-urban office developments will generally have public transport drop off points and these should be catered for in the design.

3.5.1

LOADING BAYS AND BUILDING MANAGEMENT

The loading bay should be sized to cater for the required number and size of vehicles needed to support the building. The number of vehicle trips per day can be calculated, based on the gross floor area and accepted ratios for the different uses, i.e. offices, retail, restaurant use and so on. This will confirm the number and type of loading bays required, and this, combined with the swept path analysis, will set the key dimensions of the space. In addition, calculations can confirm the size of required compactors and number of Euro Bins (once again based on gross floor area and use type). Combined with a provision for set down, recycling and storage space, will define the overall size of the loading bay.

Ensuring ease of movement between the various occupiers/uses and the loading bay is very important for usability and health and safety reasons.

It is recommended that a full waste management and servicing strategy is prepared at the outset of the project. This is especially relevant in mixed use and multi-occupier schemes and will allow the recycling strategy to be agreed early in the process.

There is no standard solution for loading bay size, layout or location. As the facility relates specifically to the size, mix of use, access to and location of the building, solutions are generally bespoke. Specialist advice should be sought at the beginning of the design process in order to consider the occupational needs and local authority requirement.

3.6 GRIDS

3.6.1 PLANNING GRID

The planning grid is the means of co-ordinating components of the structure, fabric, services and finishes. This includes the column grid, mullion spacing, ceiling layout and partition grid. The discipline of the planning grid supports ease and economy of construction and fit out. By facilitating space planning to support a range of workstyles, it will ensure flexibility and adaptability of the space in use.

3.0 / BUILDING FORM

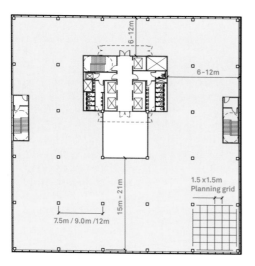

A planning grid of 1.5 m × 1.5 m is the preferred standard in the UK
This supports efficient planning of circulation and open work space and allows a range of perimeter room widths (3.0 m, 4.5 m, 6.0 m, and so on) to be fully co-ordinated with the building elements and services. Variations to 1.2 m × 1.2 m or 1.35 m × 1.35 m may be justified (these are more common in Europe than in the UK), especially where a large number of individual perimeter offices are dictated by organisational preferences.

Courtesy of Sheppard Robson

3.6.2

💧💧 9 m × 9 m grids offer the optimum weight of frames followed by 9 m × 12 m and 12 m × 12 m. Transfer structures can be introduced to irregular grid situations, but provide less flexibility than regular grids and can be more costly.

STRUCTURAL GRID

To follow through on the discipline of the planning grid, the structural grid should be a multiple of this 1.5 m dimension. To maximise flexibility, the structural grid should be as large as possible, having regard to the technical and cost constraints inherent in the selected structural material. Overall plan depth will affect the selected grid; the shallower floor plates (12–15 m) potentially being achieved in one span, while larger spans will need central columns to avoid excessive capital cost and beam depth impacting on ceiling void co-ordination.

Mixed use developments bring an added dimension to the process of grid selection. Standard office grids may not be ideal for parking areas or residential use, but if the mixed use development is office-led, suitability for office use should be the dominant deciding factor unless the addition of transfer structures is warranted.

Combinations of 7.5 m, 9 m and 12 m grids are recommended
for deep plan multi-storey buildings
Experience has shown that these combinations are efficient both
in terms of construction and cost. For shallow plan and low-rise
buildings, the smaller spans are more common, and offer
opportunities for alternative construction materials.

Perimeter columns should preferably be imbedded into or
adjacent to the external façade in order to avoid small gaps that
may need filling in as part of the fit out. Where the façade is fully
glazed the column should be pulled in by 350 mm. This enables
the space to be measured as net area while not limiting potential
fit out.

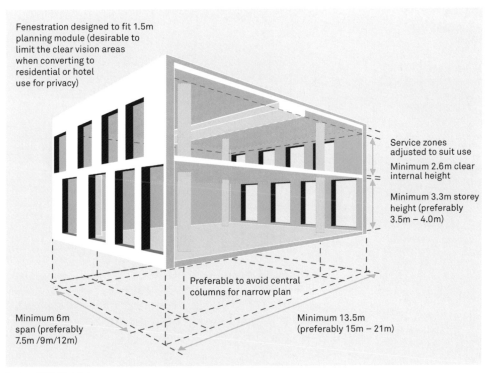

Fenestration designed to fit 1.5m
planning module (desirable to
limit the clear vision areas
when converting to residential or hotel
use for privacy)

Service zones
adjusted to suit use

Minimum 2.6m clear
internal height

Minimum 3.3m storey
height (preferably
3.5m – 4.0m)

Preferable to avoid central
columns for narrow plan

Minimum 6m
span (preferably
7.5m /9m/12m)

Minimum 13.5m
(preferably 15m – 21m)

Courtesy of 3D Reid Architecture

3.7

CIRCULATION

Percentage of primary circulation to net internal area: 15–22%

Primary circulation is the network of clear routes within the net internal area connecting all points of entry and exit and providing access to all parts of the workplace area. A nominal width of 1.5 m (co-ordinated with a 1.5 m planning grid) is preferred, though this may be reduced where it passes internal columns: the minimum width will be determined by escape considerations.

Ideally, all parts of the open workplace area should be within 7.5 m of a designed route; a plan depth greater than 15 m will therefore generally dictate two longitudinal primary circulation routes. Zones for the provision of enclosed rooms in a range of sizes should be considered in determining the circulation pattern.

The proportion of net internal area required for an efficient primary circulation network should generally lie between 15% and 22%, depending on plan depth, leaving approximately 78–85% of net useable area for planning of workplaces. While the 'user efficiency' of the space (the ratio of net useable to net internal) may be measured by an incoming occupier, a clear circulation pattern providing effective access to all workplaces should not be sacrificed in order to increase the apparent percentage of net useable area.

Secondary circulation – the space providing access for short distances within and around personal workspaces – should be included within space standards when space requirements are determined.

Initial design should consider how the space can be divided into multiple occupancies with minimal loss of lettable space. Critical in achieving this is an understanding of primary circulation and location of means of escape. See diagram opposite.

1 KINGDOM STREET, LONDON
Photographer: Edward Hill Photography

Primary and secondary circulation, and potential sub-division into
4 independent occupancies *courtesy of Sheppard Robson*

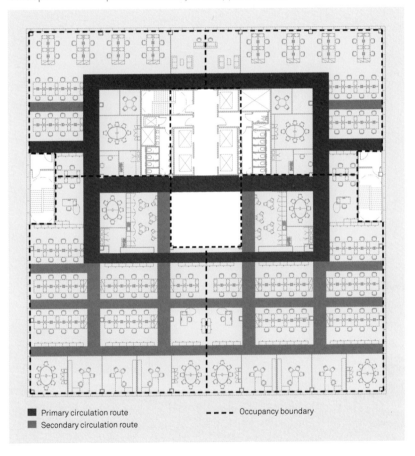

■ Primary circulation route   – – – – Occupancy boundary
■ Secondary circulation route

3.0 /

3.8

£ £ Areas available
for future plant and
risers should be planned at
the outset.

FLOOR PLATE EFFICIENCY

There are two common measures of floor plate efficiency:

Plan efficiency (NIA:GIA): the ratio of net internal area (NIA) to gross internal area (GIA) for a typical floor, for buildings up to nine storeys in height should be in the region of 80-85%

→ Wall to floor ratio (the ratio of external wall area to internal floor area). Typically, a ratio of 0.4 provides an efficient and cost effective model. If the ratio exceeds 0.4, a design review should test the design and value. The lower the ratio, the more efficient the floor plate design is in relation to the external wall area and its associated cost.

Considering efficiency purely on area ratios assists design optimisation, but equally, occupier needs must be considered. Space needs to be useful as well as efficient, that means efficient space planning for fitting out is key to creating effective space for the user, achieving efficiency of circulation routes, ease of sub-division, flexibility for various occupier fit out strategies (cellular, open plan) and dealing with setbacks and other anomolies.

Smaller floor plate (circa 750 m² or less) are generally less efficient than larger floor plates (2,500 m² or more) as the cores become disproportionately large.

The key drivers of efficiency are:
→ **The form and size of the floor plate.** Trying to achieve simple rectilinear floor plates with the principal and secondary cores located to serve the maximum floor space. Fire engineered solutions applied to this challenge can reduce the number of secondary cores, by extending means of escape distances, and should therefore be considered early in the process.

94

→ **The anticipated level of occupation.** Work to an occupancy standard that reflects the likely market needs but has the flexibility to increase during the life of the building. This will include knock-out panels for the provision of additional services, additional external plant space for heat rejection and base build WCs located and planned to allow more to be simply added to the block. Stairs should be built to the maximum anticipated floor occupancy level, because they often cannot be changed post-occupation without significant disruption to the building.

→ **The number of floors.** Tall buildings require extra lifting capacity and service for a given useable floor area (see Figure 3.2).

→ **Efficient core layouts.**

→ **Optimised façade zones.** This is achieved by reducing the thickness of the envelope to the minimum practical dimension (particularly important for urban locations). A measure of NIA to GIA is used for benchmarking purposes.

Figure 3.2 Floor plate efficiency ranges of typical multi-storey office buildings
(net: gross floor area ratios)

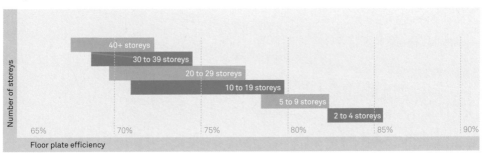

4.0 /

SUSTA

Sustainability is a recurring theme throughout this Guide. However, this Section draws together answers to the main issues that arise at the outset of a new build or refurbishment project, namely: will it be cost-effective, how should sustainability be measured, and what is the best way to ensure that sustainability targets are reached?

NABILITY

TALKING POINTS

Sustainability

Business performance

Cost & value

4.0 /

4.1

(£)(£) For every £1 that a UK
company spends on
eligible energy-saving assets
under the Enhanced Capital
Allowances (ECA) regime, the
true cost after tax is only 78p.

FURTHER READING
Eichholtz, P., Kok, N.
and Quigley, J.M., *Doing
Well By Doing Good?
Green Office Buildings*.
Working Paper No.
W08-001. University of
California, April 2008.

*Green Building Smart
Market Report*,
McGraw Hill
Construction, 2006.

*Green Building in
North America*,
Secretariat of the
Commission for
Environmental
Cooperation 2008.

*Commercial Real
Estate and the
Environment*, CoStar
Group, March 2008.

SUSTAINABILITY AND GREEN VALUE STUDIES

When it is considered that environmental sustainability, in its
simplest form, is fundamentally about minimising waste then
it becomes easier to accept that 'greener' construction can also
lead to reduced costs. If this principle is extended to lifetime
operations, then sustainability has an even clearer link to
reduced running costs.

It is well established that increased investment (perhaps in more
efficient plant or improved levels of insulation), can improve
energy efficiency and reduce running costs over the lifetime
of the building. Therefore opportunities for improving the
sustainability of the building should be considered at the earliest
possible stage in the development project (i.e. concept stage).

For owner-occupiers the case for increased capital expenditure
to bring lifetime benefits becomes a fairly simple business case.
But even for speculative development, greener construction and
even the case for enhanced more expensive designs may soon
become clearer, with the market expected to slowly place a
premium on better buildings, such as those with a BREEAM
'Excellent' rating (see below) or those with an energy
performance certificate (EPC) of grade C or better.

The Code for Sustainable Homes, and the mooted equivalent Code for Non-domestic Buildings, will place increasingly tough standards on new-build and refurbishment by the second half of the next decade. Figure 4.1 presents an overview of the likely changes to policy over the next decade, which aim to reduce the overall carbon emissions from buildings.

Figure 4.1 Changes to UK government policies relating to sustainability in the built environment

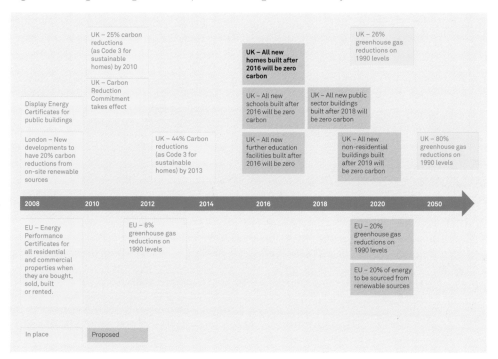

4.0 /

4.2

FURTHER READING
Pintér, L., Hardi, P.,
and Bartelmus, P.,
*Sustainable
Development
Indicators: Proposals
for a Way Forward*,
International Institute
for Sustainable
Development, 2005

MEASURING SUSTAINABILITY

Measuring sustainability is a tricky business, partly because sustainability is a broad and general concept and has always been defined in universal terms. Several types of sustainability indicators have been proposed to measure sustainability in various contexts. For example, the UN Division for Sustainable Development develops indicators for the use of national governments, but there are also indicators for financial markets, for food and agriculture, water infrastructure, etc.

For buildings, sustainability indicators are reflected in the various rating systems, self-certification schemes and government mandates that have been developed in the past two decades. These generally place a greater emphasis on the environmental than the economic and social aspects of sustainability, simply because buildings consume a substantial proportion of available resources. According to the US Green Building Council, for example, buildings account for 40% of material and energy use, 17% of freshwater withdrawal, 33% of carbon dioxide emissions (source: www.usgbc.org). However, some of these processes also incorporate social considerations, such as well-being, public realm, open space, place making etc.

The best known comprehensive systems that measure sustainability of buildings are the checklist-based voluntary schemes BREEAM (the Building Research Establishment's Environmental Assessment Method), LEED (Leadership in Energy and Environmental Design), the Comprehensive Assessment System for Building Environmental Efficiency (CASBEE), Haute qualité environnementale (HQE) and Green Star.

BREEAM and LEED are the most internationally recognised amongst these, with bespoke rating systems for international projects, such as BREEAM Europe or LEED India. CASBEE, HQE and Green Star are more popular in the countries where they were originally developed – Japan, France and Australia, respectively. Table 4.1 presents a summary of the key features of the most widely available assessment methods.

Table 4.1 Commonly used environmental assessment methods

	BREEAM	LEED	HQE	CASBEE	Green Star	Energy Performance Certificates	Display Energy Certificates	IPD Environment Code	SEEDA/ London Sustainability Checklists
Ecology	▲	★	★	★	★				◆
Water	▲	★	★	★	★			◆	◆
Waste	▲	★	★	★	★			◆	◆
Transport	▲	★	★	★	★			◆	◆
Energy: fixed services (base build)	▲	★	★	★	★	●	■	◆	◆
Energy: fixed services (occupier fit-out)	▲	★	★	★	★		■	◆	
Process energy		★						◆	
Indoor environmental quality	▲	★	★	★	★			◆	◆
Management	▲							◆	◆
Materials	▲	★	★	★	★				◆
Social issues		★							◆
Economic issues								◆	◆

● Legislative requirement for all new buildings and for all buildings being sold or let

■ Legislative requirement for existing public buildings greater than 1000 m²

▲ Voluntary, 3rd party assessed, often a UK planning requirement

★ Voluntary, 3rd party assessed

◆ Voluntary, not 3rd party assessed

Where these methods are certified by independent assessors, building developers/owners are awarded various levels of certification. These certification levels, such as BREEAM 'Outstanding' and 'Excellent' and LEED 'Platinum' are becoming increasingly recognised as hallmarks of environmental performance and valuable marketing tools.

There are also several self-certification schemes that measure sustainability in the built environment, but do not include third-party verification. Such schemes include the South East England Development Agency's (SEEDA) 'Checklist South East' or its derivative, the Mayor of London's 'London Sustainability Checklist' and the Investment Property Data (IPD) Environment Code. These assessment methods often reflect current best practice for existing buildings and for projects being currently built. They serve mostly as a check for the owner/developer's own satisfaction, and are not verified independently, thus their marketing value is limited.

4.0 / SUSTAINABILITY

FURTHER READING
*BREEAM, BRE
Environmental
and Sustainability
Standard, BES 5055:
Issue 2.0, BREEAM
Offices 2008
Assessor Manual,*
Building Research
Establishment, 2008.

*The Leadership
in Energy and
Environmental Design
(LEED) Green Building
Rating System™,* US
Green Building Council.

Although as yet there are no comprehensive assessment systems that are mandatory, BREEAM and LEED are becoming a standard expectation from the property market and local authorities in the UK and the US. This quasi-mandatory status indicates a vision from the creators of these systems that one day BREEAM and LEED become a legislative requirement. Indeed, the residential version of BREEAM – the Code for Sustainable Homes – is already mandatory for all new homes in the UK; and some states, counties and cities in the US are mandating minimum LEED requirements for buildings.

The UK Office of Government Commerce has developed a best practice tool with key performance indicators to enable departments to measure and manage their own estate performance with the aim of improving efficiency and effectiveness (available in its publication *Better Measurement: Better Management*). The data which they base their reasoning on refers to buildings in the civil estate. Techniques and standards proposed have been developed by the Investment Property Databank (IPD) for occupiers, and includes the use of the total occupancy cost code to help identify potential efficiencies. The performance framework has basic costs such as rent, rates, work station costs, space per workstation and other costs. The tool is based on three main areas: work-based productivity (functional suitability, workplace environment, facilities and downtime); environmental sustainability (energy, waste, water and pollution); and management practices and operability (conditions, health and safety). A scoring system is proposed that is based upon IPD occupiers' data set.

> Though assessment systems address important aspects of sustainability, by their very nature they simplify complex systems into an easily understandable rating.

Though assessment systems address important aspects of sustainability, by their very nature they simplify complex systems into an easily understandable rating. Rating systems differ from each other in terms of the metrics they use to measure sustainability and many of them have a reduced scope.

Although carbon emissions dominate discussions on environmental sustainability, other very important aspects – such as water consumption, ecology and materials – are frequently overlooked, both in terms of usage and waste disposal. Even low carbon designs still tend to focus on operational impacts rather than those associated with construction or embedded within the materials (i.e. 'embodied' energy, see below).

Standards such as BREEAM and LEED do cover these wider environmental aspects, and since 2008 the BREEAM family has imposed minimum standards for a variety of these, so to achieve Very Good ratings or better a building will need to demonstrate sustainability across the board, not simply score very highly in one area at the expense of others.

4.2.1

OPERATIONAL AND EMBODIED ENERGY

Measuring sustainability needs to include the following two areas of carbon use in buildings:

→ **Building performance or building performance in use.** Various assessment tools have been introduced and are still being developed to help understand how buildings perform when occupied and whether they compare to design aspirations. But following the introduction of Display Energy Certificates (DECs), it is likely that these will become the most widely used label for building performance in use.

→ **Embodied energy and full building life cycle.** Regulations and most analytical tools currently focus on building performance, tending to ignore the carbon 'embodied' within the building and the impacts of construction (for example, the carbon emissions generated as a result of energy expended to extract, process, transport and use the materials that make up the building). However, as operational energy efficiency improves, the embodied energy will form a greater percentage of the lifecycle total (see Figure 4.2), and it will become increasingly important to address this and to understand how trade-offs between embodied energy and operational carbon can advance cost-effectiveness. (See Section 4.3.2 Materials specification.)

Figure 4.2 Actual operational carbon versus embedded carbon

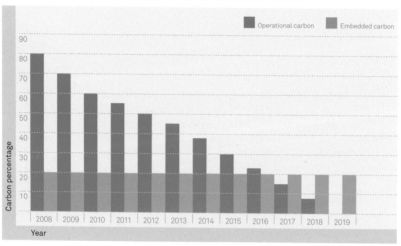

4.2.2

FURTHER READING
*Energy Consumption
Guide 19* (ECON 19),
Carbon Trust

BUILDING REGULATIONS PART L

There has been a major impact on office design as a result of European legislation – the Energy Performance of Buildings Directive (EPBD). The EPBD has been introduced (transposed) in a slightly different way in the UK regions due to the subsequent introduction of changes to:

→ The Building Regulations in England and Wales Approved Document L2A Conservation of Fuel and Power in new buildings other than dwellings (see www.communites.gov.uk/planningandbuilding)
→ The Building Regulations in Northern Ireland (Part F2) (see www.dfpni.gov.uk/br-legislation)
→ The Scottish Technical Handbook, Section 6, Energy (see www.sbsa.gov.uk/tech_handbooks).

The Building Regulations in Northern Ireland are very similar to England and Wales with slight differences in the fuel carbon emissions. In Scotland there are slight differences in the U-value standards of the building envelope fabric and the requirements for air-tightness testing.

Each revision of Part L sets new minimum standards for carbon emissions for base building installations. Best practice and exemplar commercial offices are generally 10–15% better than the current standard. (Note: for naturally ventilated and heated buildings, the percentage reduction in the 2006 revisions to Part L2A of the Building Regulations is 23%.)

Part L2A only takes into account the regulated carbon emissions from the building's fixed installations, which typically accounts for about 50–60% of the total carbon emissions. The difference is attributable to the carbon emissions from the 'in-use' energy consumed by office equipment (computers, photocopiers, catering equipment, etc.), which occur once the building is occupied. Although Part L2A ignores 'in-use' energy, it cannot be excluded from the overall energy strategy for the development, especially when assessing local planning requirements.

MARSHAM STREET (THE HOME OFFICE) LONDON
Copyright: Terry Farrell and Partners. Photographer: Steve Cadman

The Building Regulations are seen as an important part of the UK government's strategy for reducing carbon emissions. The Department for Communities and Local Government (CLG) is actively exploring a 'road map' that will lead to a regulatory requirement for zero carbon buildings. Figure 4.3 shows the likely 'road map' for Part L carbon emissions. (See also Appendix A2: Statutory regulations.)

Figure 4.3 Building Regulations Part L: carbon emissions 'road map'

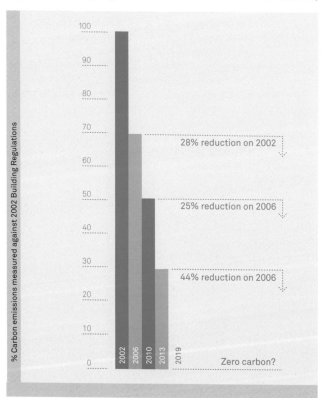

4.2.3

ENERGY PERFORMANCE CERTIFICATES

The introduction of Energy Performance Certificates (EPCs) is a requirement of Article 7 of the EPBD. EPCs have been introduced for the construction, sale or rent (let) of buildings. These certificates contain the Asset Rating for the building and have to be renewed at least every ten years and be accompanied by a list of recommendations (the Recommendations Report) on how to improve the building's energy performance.

An EPC is a theoretical benchmark produced using the same software tool that calculates the Part L rating. As with Part L, the EPC assessment does not calculate 'in-use' energy and carbon emissions. The way that certificates are produced and calculated varies across the UK and therefore certificates for buildings in the different devolved administrations are not directly comparable.

Table 4.2 Carbon emissions calculations in the UK

Nation	Regulation	Scale used for EPC
England and Wales	Regulations 2007 Statutory Instrument (SI) 2007/991, amended by SI 2007/1669, SI 2007/3302 and SI 2008/647 documentation	Scale based upon a CO_2 ratio of the building's emissions compared with a reference building, and is therefore a dimensionless scale with the EPC rating ranging from A = 0–25 and G = 150+
Northern Ireland	As England and Wales	As England and Wales
Scotland	Energy Performance of Buildings (Scotland) Regulations 2008	Scale based upon kilograms of CO_2 emissions per square meter of floor area, based upon standard occupancy profiles. (The Scottish EPC scale ranges from A (1–15 most efficient) to G (100+ least efficient)

FURTHER READING
BCO Guide to Green Incentives, 2009

Courtesy of Department for
Communities and Local Government

→ Part L: 2006 compliant
air-conditioned and mechanically
ventilated buildings should target
a 'C' rating.
→ Naturally ventilated or mixed mode
buildings should target 'B'.
→ To achieve BREEAM 'Excellent', an
EPC rating of 40 or less is required
(B Rating).

4.2.4

DISPLAY ENERGY CERTIFICATES (DECS)

FURTHER READING
Improving the energy efficiency of our buildings - A guide to Display Energy Certificates and advisory reports for public buildings, Department for Communities and Local Government Guide (ISBN: 978-1-8511-2981-2)

Display Energy Certificates (DECs) show a record of
how a building has actually performed. DECs are required for
buildings over 1000 m² occupied by public authorities and by
institutions providing public services to a large number of
persons (and therefore frequently visited).

Courtesy of Department for
Communities and Local Government

The ratings shown in a DEC are known
as Operational Ratings and have to be
renewed each year. They are based on
up to three years worth of actual
energy consumption data, and the
certificate must be accompanied by an
advisory report, which is valid for up to
seven years.

In Scotland Display Energy Certificates
are not used; EPCs are displayed
instead.

4.3

DESIGN APPROACH

Offices, whether located on business parks or in urban areas, share many common core requirements, such as occupant density, comfort requirements, lighting, heating, cooling and ventilation. With careful consideration of site location, orientation, form and layout, the designer can take advantage of solar gain, shading, local wind effects and daylight in order to create a more 'passive' building and reduce its environmental impact. To maximise use of natural systems, internal spaces should be zoned according to heating, cooling, light and ventilation requirements. Reduced reliance on mechanical and electrical systems will result in lower operational costs and lower carbon emissions.

Design decisions such as the overall form of the building, the depth and height of rooms, and the size and location of windows, can have a great impact on the eventual energy use of the building. There are also clear benefits for the occupants if the building and site are both planned to promote the effective use of daylight and a sense of connection to the natural environment.

CHISWICK PARK
Copyright: Stanhope PLC by Hufton + Crowe

Equally, it is widely recognised that, while new build has generally moved rapidly towards the low/ zero carbon goal, the greatest challenge we face as an industry is the stock of buildings that already exist. Refurbishment projects, while generally being inherently more environmentally desirable, must give due consideration to the sustainability agenda. The integration of innovative features, materials or systems can dramatically improve the environmental performance of an existing building. Operational targets that focus on improved lighting, selection of finishes and materials, comfort conditions, better control and reductions in the energy use of the building should be set.

4.3.1

FURTHER READING
BREEAM for Offices,
BRE 2008

SETTING A CLEAR TARGET

BREEAM Rating: All new and refurbished offices should aim for a minimum of 'Very Good' and best practice is to achieve 'Excellent'

A new category of 'Outstanding' is available for BREEAM 2008 onwards, which is intended to promote innovation in sustainable design.

To achieve BREEAM 'Excellent' an EPC rating of 40 or less is required (B rating). An EPC rating of 'B' may require natural or mixed mode ventilation and a contribution from on-site renewables.

To achieve a successful result, it is essential to choose the environmental assessment method at an early stage of the design process and to appointment an approved assessor. Credits to be targeted (and any pre-requisites for the target rating) need to be identified, communicated and explained to the design team as early as possible.

4.3.2

The minimisation of waste during construction starts with good design, with thought being directed to ways of reducing waste and reusing and recycling any demolition resources.

MATERIALS SPECIFICATION

The extraction, production and transportation of materials is responsible for a significant proportion of the construction sector's environmental impact, and although the legislative drivers have been slow to arrive, there is increasing interest in how the impacts can be lessened. The Aggregates Levy and Landfill Tax have encouraged an increase in on-site recycling of demolition material, but there is more that can be done.

The selection and specification of materials is an important factor in an office building, and should consider aesthetic, functional, durability, indoor environment, local and global environmental impacts. Preference should be given to materials that are from sustainable sources.

The 'reuse and recycle' mantra relies upon a demand for the recyclates and specifiers have a role in encouraging recycling and enhancing the supply chain. As such, it is likely to be increasingly important to require a minimum percentage amount of recycled material within new products. The government-backed Waste and Resources Action Programme (WRAP) recommends that a minimum of 10% recycled building content by value should be a target (during construction).

Creating a sustainable building may include:
→ Choosing sustainably sourced timber (e.g. FSC, PEFC or CSA), which is now widely available and should not attract a cost premium
→ Changing the concrete specification, where appropriate and suitable, not only requires less material and so reduces costs, it also reduces the embodied carbon content of the building
→ Using low-emitting and rapidly renewable materials internally can improve indoor air quality, creating a healthier and more productive workspace
→ Ordering materials in quantities and sizes that suit the needs of the development (why order and pay for more than you need only to pay again to throw away the wastage?).

As the carbon emissions associated with the operation of buildings falls, the significance of the carbon emissions associated with producing building materials and components becomes more important. Therefore it is important to choose materials with the lowest possible embodied energy, and the key elements – particularly external walls, windows, floors and roofs – should be environmentally friendly. Developers and their design teams should make decisions based on a balance between whole-life cost and environmental impact. Environmental assessment methods such as BREEAM and LEED give guidance on the suitability of materials.

4.3.3

INDOOR COMFORT

All offices share the common requirements for thermal comfort, ventilation and lighting, all of which can be fully or partially provided with passive systems, helping to reduce energy use and carbon emissions.

It is important that the end product meets the need of the occupiers to provide cost-effective, comfortable, secure and efficient space

The main demand of the modern office in a city centre will be for cooling due to a variety of factors such as incidental heat gains from people and equipment and the rise in external temperatures. The selection of inherently low carbon cooling strategies (for example, thermal mass, phase change materials, ground source cooling, nearby bodies of water and absorption chillers using waste energy streams) compatible with the comfort and quality aspirations of the client will be crucial to the energy efficiency of a development and in meeting future government performance targets. The starting point should therefore be to seek to minimise the use of energy through passive measures, harnessing what is free and benign and minimising the environmental impact.

Air-conditioning can provide year-round stable thermal conditions, and the carbon emissions associated with mechanical comfort control can be significantly reduced, providing the building is designed to maximise its use of 'free cooling' and to work in tandem with passive cooling strategies.

Designing to achieve highly energy-efficient and low carbon buildings requires an evaluation of the combined effects of building form and fabric, engineering and control systems, occupancy behaviour and climate. Modern low-cost computer analysis allows designers to create 'virtual' buildings and investigate their 'in use' performance. Computer modelling should therefore be used to investigate and optimise the interplay between these parameters and to explore alternative design approaches.

The combination and consideration of all these factors can highlight opportunities to improve energy efficiency which can then be incorporated into the building from the early stages of design. However, it is important that the end product meets the need of the occupiers to provide cost-effective, comfortable, secure and efficient space.

4.3.4

REGIONAL VARIATIONS

GREEN PARK, READING
Copyright: Ecotricity

A more sustainable building needs to work within the local microclimate. Solutions for an office in a city centre can be very different to a non-urban greenfield site. Rainfall, sunshine hours, wind speeds and air temperatures can all change the economic viability of building systems. For example, the viability of a wind turbine is far greater in the Scottish highlands than in central London. Rain water harvesting in the Lake District will collect more water than one in East Anglia (where the need is actually greater). A solar thermal hot water collector in Cornwall has the ability to generate more energy than one in Cumbria.

Location matters and a sustainable office will need to work with the opportunities offered by the unique ecological and climate variations of its own particular location.

Sustainability is about fitting in with the local environment, and ecological and transport issues must be considered along with the need for the building to use less water and energy.

4.0 /

4.4

(£)(£) Providing low or zero
carbon technologies
as part of a development
may increase capital cost,
but will reduce carbon
emissions and running costs.

ENERGY STRATEGY

Increasing reliance on information technology has transformed
the workplace, driving denser occupation and placing heavy
demands on building services. Yet modern office buildings must
remain pleasant to use and strive towards sustainability; their
building services installations must provide comfortable
conditions and reduce harmful effects on the environment.

Functionality and comfort have long been important factors in
office specification. However, climate change and sustainability
have become key influences on building design and are the
motivation behind much recent EU and UK legislation and
planning policy, from the introduction of Energy Performance
Certificates, to the Greater London Authority's London Plan.

BISHOPS SQUARE, SPITALFIELDS
Copyright: Hammerson

Figure 4.5 Step by step approach to minimising carbon emissions

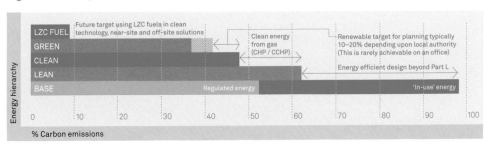

Typically, for a new development or a refurbishment project, a bespoke energy statement should be prepared. This will assess the benefits of a range of carbon reduction and low or zero carbon (LZC) approaches (see Figure 4.5), and allows an energy strategy to be established as the basis for the remainder of the building design. The energy statement may also form a supporting part of a planning application to demonstrate how the building is to meet local authority energy and sustainability targets.

The energy strategy should demonstrate how the development will apply the 'lean, clean and green' philosophy to reducing carbon emissions. The energy strategy should explore how the building will:

→ Meet Part L of the Building Regulations
→ Achieve target energy performance ratings
→ Meet local authority planning requirements.

The 'lean, clean and green' hierarchy (illustrated overleaf) should be applied to the energy strategy, setting priorities for the selection of carbon saving measures.

→ The first step in the hierarchy is the lean approach and this is where significant energy and hence carbon emissions can be saved by the application of a good quality, holistic and inter-disciplinary design approach.
→ The second step is the efficient supply of clean energy.
→ The third is the most difficult to achieve and that is the use of renewable green energy.

The 'lean, clean and green' energy strategy

LEAN ↓

Eliminate or reduce loads through passive means – maximise daylight, minimise heating and cooling.
Loads should be minimised through measures such as shading, beneficial orientation, free cooling, etc., to reduce the reliance on mechanical systems, or potentially eliminate them. Make the most of energy that is consumed – specify high-efficiency systems and components.

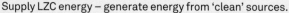

CLEAN ↓

Supply LZC energy – generate energy from 'clean' sources.
'Clean' energy may be supplied from district heating schemes fed from waste-to-heat-and-power plants or from combined heat and power (CHP) plants. Although not zero carbon in their impact, clean power sources maximise the use of energy from any given source. CHP plants are particularly suited to mixed-use developments where they can take advantage of varied demand and diversities.

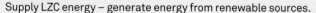

GREEN ↓

Supply LZC energy – generate energy from renewable sources.
Energy may also be supplied from renewable (zero carbon) sources such as biomass, photovoltaic cells, geothermal sources, solar thermal panels, wind, and in some cases potentially from wave power.

4.4.1

The inclusion of some form of renewable technology is encouraged by the Scottish Technical Standards and Building Regulations, BREEAM and local planning guidance. Renewables should be considered only after the design has been developed to reduce the base energy load and the options considered should be appropriate to energy profile, future use and context.

LOCAL PLANNING REQUIREMENTS

Planning Policy Statement 22 (England/Wales) and Scottish Planning Policy 6 set out the national policies for planning with regard to renewable energy. Northern Ireland is currently developing PPS 18 which is in draft format.

The policies set out in these documents form the basis of renewable energy planning policies for regional planning bodies in the preparation of regional spatial strategies and for the Mayor's Spatial Development Strategy in London likewise by local planning authorities in the preparation of local development documents. They may also be material to decisions on individual planning applications.

Local planning authority requirements vary both in extent and application of the national planning policies with renewable requirements ranging from 10–20%. Often it is impractical to achieve the requirements in pure 'green' renewable technology. In such circumstances, a negotiation with the planning authority usually results in a compromise involving the practical application of the 'lean', 'clean' and 'green' hierarchy (described previously), i.e., designing the lowest practical carbon footprint for the building, resulting in a smaller renewables requirement.

4.4.2

LOW AND ZERO CARBON (LZC) OPTIONS

When preparing the energy strategy, the most suitable technologies should be fully assessed for whole life carbon emission savings, capital investment and ongoing operational costs/savings. This information will inform the strategy as to which solution is the most appropriate to meet the legislative, local planning and corporate responsibility requirements. Investment in such technologies can be significant. Appendix A7: Low and zero carbon technologies, reviews the most popular clean and green technologies that are considered suitable for office buildings.

4.0 /

4.5

CONSTRUCTION AND HAND-OVER

From material extraction, processing, component assembly, transport and construction, to maintenance and disposal, construction products have an environmental impact over their entire life cycle.

Contractors should be encouraged to work extensively with local suppliers to minimise transportation requirements and utilise the local skills base. Also ensure that waste of materials is avoided during both the design and construction stages, exploring opportunities to use locally available materials and products, salvaged materials and recycling or reusing materials from the existing site or building.

Site waste management plans (SWMPs) are now mandatory in England for any scheme, refurbishment or new-build, valued at over £300,000. SWMPs are not yet mandatory in other parts of the UK, although many companies implement them as an example of best practice, and many local authorities in Scotland are advocating their use. The aim is to consider waste at every stage of a project, to reduce waste production and then to re-use or recycle any waste that is produced, minimising the need for landfill.

4.5.1

FURTHER READING
Guide to Post-Occupancy Evaluation,
BCO 2007

POST-OCCUPANCY EVALUATION

It is important to keep in touch with the way the building is used and performs on completion as a continuous learning tool for all parties.

To learn from projects it is important to monitor the building performance over the first 24 months of occupancy, to allow the occupiers to understand the controls and user requirements and make necessary adjustments. Good design will always look at how offices can be operated and maintained over the design life. Schemes such as 'Soft Landings' will help with this process (see Section 9.3). The BCO Guide on Post-Occupancy Evaluation provides an in-depth guide on what needs to be covered.

DASHWOOD HOUSE, LONDON
Photographer: Paul Grundy

4.6

FURTHER READING
*Definition of zero
carbon homes
and non-domestic
buildings*, DCLG 2008

FUTURE-PROOFING

Provision should be considered for the future introduction of low and zero carbon (LZC) and other technologies as they become available. For instance, space could be left for a fuel cell driven from a future hydrogen distribution system or provision made for existing equipment to be able to operate on biogas, if such a system is planned in the locality.

Carbon emission standards become more stringent with each new revision of legislation and they are already close to the limit of technology available for building services. The government has declared its aim to make new office buildings carbon neutral from 2019 (see Figure 4.1) and for this aim to be achieved fundamental changes must be made. Two approaches are available:

→ **Change the specification of the building.** For example, reduce loads in the building by limiting small power availability or reducing occupation density; make natural ventilation possible by limiting the plan depth and removing limits on noise levels, relaxing temperature and humidity set points. This type of approach may affect the viability of a building because it will restrict the use of the office and will limit the number of people who can be accommodated on a given building plot for urban buildings. Designing an urban building for natural ventilation could reduce the net lettable area available and reduce the quality of space that is created.

→ **Procure LZC energy from off-site sources.** This approach of offsetting carbon emissions would allow dense development to continue, but is not currently acceptable to statutory bodies who fear that energy supply arrangements could be changed too easily by an occupier, allowing reversion to lower cost, higher carbon sources for example taking power from wind farms; cooling and/or heating from community networks or waste-to-energy plants.

FURTHER READING
Expected life of
plant and equipment,
see: CIBSE Guide M,
*Maintenance
Engineering and
Management,*
Appendix 13.
Comprehensive
guidance on life cycle
and life cycle costs:
BS ISO 15686 parts
1–3, 5, 6 & 8.

At the time of writing this document, the Department for
Communities and Local Government has issued a consultation
document which asks whether off-site energy production
could be used as the lowest hierarchy in measures to achieve
zero carbon.

Energy consumption and carbon emissions will become
increasingly important as fuel costs rise and legislation imposes
penalties for pollution. As long as a developer or occupier has a
long term view, it is likely that operational costs will start to
dominate the life cycle cost and will lead to more energy efficient
and easily maintainable systems, although these may not have
the lowest capital outlay.

All parties involved in commercial offices are now becoming
increasingly aware of the environmental effects of the buildings
that we occupy – now more than ever this will have a major effect
on building choice.

If the client and design team consider sustainability from the
start of a project, then its impact upon the cost of construction
will be minimised.

BISHOPS SQUARE, LONDON
Copyright: Hammerson

5.0 / ENVELO

The building envelope represents one of the three largest constituents of a building, alongside structure and services. All three are intrinsically linked in terms of integrated performance and buildability, so it is essential to consider the interplay between each of these three aspects at every iteration of the design process.

PE

TALKING POINTS

Sustainability

Business performance

Cost & value

5.0 /

5.1

£€ Increased acoustic performance can attract significant cost premiums, especially where elevations are in close proximity to high density transport infrastructure.

FURTHER READING
Design & Procurement Pre-Assessment Estimator, BREEAM Offices 2006 (www.breeam.org)

FIRST PRINCIPLES

The envelope provides an interface between the controlled internal environment of an office building and the variable external climate. Thus façade designs and performance specifications must be developed in tandem with the building services design strategy in order to contribute to reducing the building's energy consumption for cooling, heating and lighting, while also achieving necessary daylighting levels.

Envelope costs vary with complexity and form, and should be tailored to reflect the property's potential investment value. Solutions may range from prefabricated (unitised) curtain wall systems (typically used in a 'sealed box' development for a city-centre commercial office) to a variety of site-built systems for smaller out-of-town locations, possibly with opening windows for natural ventilation.

While non-urban office buildings are typically low-rise and offer the possibility of employing traditional construction methods and natural ventilation, city centre buildings usually (at least historically) require a high degree of prefabrication and need to accommodate more onerous performance challenges, such as enhanced acoustic criteria. The trend towards mixed-use developments adds complexity by forcing the building envelope design to incorporate diverse performance requirements, such as the need for privacy and opening vents for residential accommodation.

The environmental strategy for the whole building needs to be determined before the services design can commence, which in turn needs to be aligned with realistically achievable performance criteria for the envelope.

The type of construction for the building envelope is, to some degree, dictated by the value of the development. Small developments can achieve attractive and individual solutions by employing proprietary systems in a creative way.

Apart from the construction method and performance requirements, the choice of materials has a major impact on the specification. Materials such as glass, aluminium and various natural stones have been used for many years and their properties, detailing and procurement are well understood. However, a number of materials that are either new (e.g. gold-coloured finish on copper sheeting), or were not previously used for commercial/office buildings (such as timber cladding or recycled glass panels), are less familiar and will require time and financial resources to do the necessary research. It is important to note that such research may result in amendments to the client's brief, or the ultimate rejection of a material with potential impacts on budget, programme or whole-life strategy for the building.

The design of the building envelope must ensure acceptable levels of thermal comfort and control the risk of condensation occurring. Large areas with low surface temperatures can cause discomfort by radiant cooling or by creating cold down-draughts. This can be of particular concern for façades with large glazed areas such as entrance lobbies, or where desks are placed close to the perimeter of the building.

8, FITZROY STREET, LONDON
Copyright: Hufton + Crowe

5.0 /

ENVELOPE

5.2

BUILDING ENVELOPE SYSTEM SOLUTIONS

5.2.1

UNITISED CURTAIN WALLING

A 1.5 m planning module represents the most efficient solution for a unitised curtain wall, in terms of capital cost and installation methodology. Unitised 'elements' (1.5 m wide, storey height), transported via service hoists and installed from the floor plates require no special external access equipment. The unitised elements are gravity loaded at each floor level and normally hung. These systems are generally capable of accommodating live load slab deflections of circa 12 mm which needs to be added to fabrication and installation tolerances.

Unitised curtain walling elements of 3.0 m wide can be built by a number of specialist contractors, and involve steel reinforcement or a steel strong-back construction. However, access is generally required from outside, thus increasing the risk of damage as elements are lifted outbound of curtain walling previously installed to lower floors. The unit cost of such systems is higher.

Panellised elements of larger widths are possible – potentially 9.0 m wide and storey height – though these are rarely used due to their cost.

Stacking from ground level or hanging curtain walling from roof level are options suitable for low rise buildings, although these methods can also be beneficial for special areas of larger buildings such as multi-storey entrance lobbies.

5.2.2

STICK SYSTEMS

Curtain walls built as stick systems accommodate lower live load deflections than unitised systems, with permissible deflections typically being less than 5 mm. Stick systems are more appropriate for low rise than tall buildings, due to the need for external access equipment during the construction phase.

126

5.2.3

RAINSCREEN SYSTEMS

Rainscreen systems comprise an outer skin that protects a ventilated cavity, with insulation between it and an inner backing wall. Material choices for the outer skin are numerous, including natural stone, ceramic, timber, metal or fibre cement panels and recycled glass.

The inner skin can be traditional blockwork/concrete (necessitating external access for installation) or unitised/stick system curtain walling.

Pre-assembling rainscreen cladding onto unitised curtain walling panels enables more thorough quality control (off site), as well as the advantages of unitised systems mentioned above. Disadvantages include increased transport costs and the pronounced jointing pattern which may not suit the architectural intent. Alternatively, rainscreens can be mounted onto large pre-cast concrete panels, thus reducing the numbers of joints.

5.2.4

PRE-CAST CONCRETE PANELS

There are two main options for pre-cast concrete building envelope solutions:

→ Large format panels, which possess the same characteristics and interaction with primary structure as panellised curtain walling, albeit with additional imposed loadings caused by the weight of concrete
→ Individual column and beam solutions, which create complex interfaces that rely heavily on the quality of the site workmanship.

Pre-cast concrete panels can have a multitude of finishes, such as etching or cast-in patterns, and can incorporate cast-in materials such as bricks, tiles and natural stone. The latter method greatly reduces the installation programme by avoiding scaffolding and the time-consuming process of hand-setting stones or laying bricks.

5.0 / ENVELOPE

5.2.5

DRY WALLS

For developments with less onerous performance requirements and/or where the construction programme allows, dry wall façade solutions could be adopted. Such systems are designed to accommodate a variety of rainscreen facing materials, and either ribbon and/or punched hole windows. Movement joints must be accommodated at each floor level and are generally similar to those experienced by unitised curtain walling. This solution requires external access for installation.

5.3

DESIGN CONSIDERATIONS

5.3.1

ACCOMMODATING WIND PRESSURES

Consider wind tunnel testing at the same time as wind environmental impact testing in order to have relevant data in place for building envelope design.

Building envelope solutions must be designed to accommodate project-specific dynamic wind pressures, which are calculated using guidance within BS6399 Part 2, in conjunction with published wind speeds pertinent to the specific location, topography and building shape.

Although BS6399 Part 2 can be used as a guide for calculating wind pressures for tall and complex-shaped buildings, the resulting loads are often more onerous than necessary. It is therefore advisable to commission wind tunnel testing for such buildings to establish the true dynamic wind pressures. The results often make more efficient building envelope design solutions possible, potentially reducing costs.

FURTHER READING
Code of practice for wind loads
BS 6399: Part 2, 1997

5.3.2

FURTHER READING
*Standard for
Systemised Building
Envelopes,* CWCT 2005

WEATHER PERFORMANCE (WATER TIGHTNESS AND AIR PERMEABILITY)

Weather performance requirements, in terms of water tightness and air permeability criteria, are defined in the Centre for Window and Cladding Technology's (CWCT) Standard for Systemised Building Envelopes. Where bespoke curtain walling systems are used, the CWCT standard specifies testing methods. Alternatively, if a proprietary curtain walling system is to be adopted, it should possess independently accredited, CWCT-compliant testing certification in order to affirm performance attributes without the need for project specific testing.

It should be noted that doors within curtain walling, particularly those with flush thresholds (often necessary for disabled access), are generally unable to meet the water tightness and air permeability criteria, thus modified test pressures or testing methods will be necessary.

5.3.3

Natural ventilation represents an opportunity to reduce energy consumption. However, in the main this would apply to non-urban developments where air and noise conditions are conducive to such a strategy.

There is a cost premium for opening windows, which becomes greater where motorisation (e.g. for night time purging) is required.

INFLUENCE OF M&E STRATEGY

Building envelope performance criteria vary, depending on the mechanical and electrical (M&E) strategy developed for a specific project, i.e. the selection of fan coils, chilled beams, displacement solutions, etc.

Speculative development incorporating 'mixed mode' is very rare at present, because the whole building cost has to accommodate the cost of a mechanical ventilation strategy as well as a building envelope solution that is upgraded to be suitable for natural ventilation.

| 5.3.4 | INTERACTION WITH PRIMARY STRUCTURE |

Building frame movement and tolerances affect the design of the connections and jointing of the building envelope. Column grids and floor-to-floor heights also influence the choice of building envelope solutions. (See Section 6.1.4)

Early co-ordination is therefore essential, because the primary structure design should accommodate the building envelope design, rather than vice versa – notably in relation to permissible live load deflections where panels are supported off the slab edge.

Almost without exception, it is better to provide extra stiffness to the structural frame around the building perimeter in order to limit movement in the building envelope, rather than designing the frame to minimum code requirements and for the cladding to accommodate larger movements or, at worst, involve expensive retrofitting on site.

For multi-storey and, in particular for tall and slender buildings, storey drift and torsion under the affect of wind load need to be assessed regarding their impact on the building envelope and its jointing system.

| 5.3.5 | BLAST ENHANCEMENT |

FURTHER READING
BCO Security Guide, 2009

Clients may specify that the building envelope must be 'blast enhanced'. To design this, it is essential to clarify the anticipated blast type, bomb weight and its proximity to the building and what failure mode would be acceptable. For example, it is typically considered an acceptable business risk that glass breaks, but not that it detaches from its framing/anchorage. Depending on the type of blast and failure mode the additional base build cost for the enhancement may be relatively low if incorporated at an early design stage.

5.4   ENERGY PERFORMANCE

The direct link between the building envelope's performance and energy consumption is reflected in the Building Regulations Approved Document Part L. In order to keep within the overall allowable levels of carbon emissions for the building stipulated in Part L, the heating and cooling loads (for air-conditioned buildings) need to be limited. Maximum energy gains and losses through the façade are influenced by shading factors (G-values), control of heat loss (U-values) and air leakage rates result.

MOOR HOUSE, LONDON
Photographer: Will Pryce

5.4.1

FURTHER READING
Building Regulations
Approved Document
Part L2A

AIRTIGHTNESS

Performance requirements and test procedures
for the completed building envelope are described in
CIBSE TN23: Testing Buildings for Air Leakage (2000) and
BSEN 13829.

For best practice, the permissible air leakage rate for the whole
building should not be more than 3.5 $m^3/hr/m^2$ ($7m^3/hr/m^2$ for
naturally ventilated buildings) at 50 Pa test pressure differential

This value does
not translate directly into
performance requirements
for façades, which can achieve
much lower values, but the
overall building performance
is directly influenced by
interfaces with roofs, soffits,
opening elements and
between different wall types.
It is therefore important to
consider specific areas at
risk of air leakage, such as
interfaces between different
envelope elements, non-
rebated doors, smoke
ventilations paths, and
so on, before setting the
performance requirements
for individual construction
elements and junction details.

Performance requirements
for curtain wall are defined in
the Centre for Windows and
Cladding Technology (CWCT)
standard for curtain walling.

BANKSIDE
Photographer: Paul Grundy

5.4.2

To achieve responsiveness to climatic variations, solar control is a key deliverable in the building envelope design. Adjustable external shading is recognised to be the most energy-efficient solution, although it can add to the complexity of the construction, operation and maintenance of the building.

The most cost-effective building envelope solutions entail a single wall system with high performance coated glass and potentially increased areas of solidity, including deeper spandrel zones. Introducing brise soleil or other external shading devices adds cost.

SOLAR GAIN

The building envelope should be capable of reacting to seasonal climatic conditions. For example, in winter months solar gain might be considered to be of benefit by providing passive solar heating, whereas in summer months solar gain must be controlled to prevent overheating and discomfort to building users.

Options to be considered:
→ External shading increases the overall depth of the façade and affects cost, while constituting a strong visual element that needs to be integrated into the architectural design.
→ Fixed external shading is typically less efficient, but involves lower capital and operating cost.
→ Shading provided by high-performance coatings or fritting on glass can provide good efficiency for the lowest additional cost in use and capital expenditure.

Reducing the glazing area by introducing additional solidity is an alternative solution that potentially reduces or obviates the need for external shading devices, without being detrimental to solar control performance. For example, glass below 800 mm above floor level does not contribute useful daylight, but increases solar gain, so could be substituted by spandrel panels.

Glare-control blinds are usually required for all glazed areas in an office development – irrespective of building envelope solutions (including those with external shading or double wall ventilated cavity solutions) – to provide visual comfort for building users. They do not effectively contribute to the reduction of solar gains unless they are in a ventilated cavity.

5.0 /

ENVELOPE

5.5

£ Consider approaching 'total envelope' specialist contractors to evolve a single package solution, thus managing risk (multiple trades to manage) and interface detailing between different wall type materials, windows, etc.

DESIGN LIFE, SERVICE LIFE, REPLACEMENT AND RECYCLING

The building envelope should function for at least 25 years without requiring major maintenance. After this period, refurbishment is usually necessary and it is then likely to provide a further 20–25 years of service life. Insulated glass units (IGUs) should not require replacement within the first 20–25 years, after which time the hermetic seals will have reached the end of their expected life and occurrence of condensation within the glass cavity becomes a risk.

Depending on climatic conditions and the precise material specification, external gaskets usually require replacing after 20–25 years and liquid applied sealants after 15–20 years.

For opening windows, doors and any other moving parts, a maintenance strategy which ensures that systems are regularly checked, adjusted and lubricated will maximise life expectancy.

Careful consideration should be given to material selection and component dimensions to ensure that replacement components are available at reasonable cost, within sensible lead times, and can be installed without time-consuming and costly installation methods.

Although aluminium is recyclable, it is currently not possible to attain the necessary quality levels required of new extrusions. However, recycling should be specified for aluminium profiles that are removed from buildings, either during demolition or refurbishment activity. The same recycling criteria should also be applied to glass, and potentially for other components including concrete and natural stone.

5.5.1

CLEANING AND MAINTENANCE

All building envelope design solutions must include suitable access for cleaning (inside and outside), maintenance, and replacement of damaged components.

A cleaning and maintenance strategy should be developed during initial design development, and access equipment should be commensurate with the building size, form and shape. This could include roof-mounted motorised gantries, access cradles, mobile elevated working platforms, or cherry pickers. For tall buildings, cradles require restraint via the building envelope at approximately eight storey intervals.

Special consideration needs to be given to roof lights or other horizontal glass surfaces. The Health & Safety Executive does not generally approve walk-on glass and a detailed risk assessment is usually required. (See Appendix A3: Health and safety.)

Replacement of small, light items can often be achieved from cleaning cradles. It is not usually economical to design cleaning equipment to be used for replacement of large, heavy items such as glass units. Larger items generally require the use of lorry-mounted cranes from ground level, or the temporary rigging of separate larger capacity crane devices at roof level.

Access equipment that is selected for cleaning and maintenance activities can affect the appearance of skylines, roof and terrace loadings, the shape, detailing and materials used for the façade, and the space planning and landscaping at the base of the building.

5.6

COSTS

The building envelope typically accounts for 15–25% of a building's construction cost.

Cost is influenced by system design, the materials chosen, the manufacturing process employed, the complexity of the installation process, and market conditions. Approximate proportions of these elements, for a typical glazed aluminium curtain wall construction on a medium to large building are:

→ 25% design, overheads and profit
→ 30% materials
→ 30% production
→ 15% installation.

Cost is influenced by:
→ The choice of materials, finishes and glass restraint methods
→ Design solutions that are deliverable by as wide a range of specialist contractors as possible
→ Use of proprietary façade systems in order to minimise design, testing time and cost
→ Procurement method.

Since April 2008, external solar shading as an integral feature is eligible for tax relief.

5.7

REFURBISHMENT PROJECTS

In refurbishment projects where the envelope has reached or is approaching the end of system or component life, envelope options are generally:

→ Retain and refinish the existing framing system and replace insulated glass units (IGUs), panels, seals, ironmongery, etc.
→ Remove the existing building envelope in total and replace with a new system.

A detailed specialist condition survey should consider the existing façade, in order to assess the suitability of retaining some or all of the cladding system, its fixing and support systems. Standards of design, performance criteria and installation methodologies have improved with time and it is possible that the existing system might not be able to be refurbished to current standards and expectations.

The need for façade renewal is not only restricted to performance; it is often part of a larger scope to remodel and re-brand a building where the appearance and quality of the building become important influences upon the scope of work.

Façade renewal is often part of a larger scope to remodel and re-brand a building where the appearance and quality of the building become important influences upon the scope of work.

5.8

FURTHER READING
Code for Sustainable
Homes, BRE 2007

POTENTIAL FUTURE DEVELOPMENTS

Façade design is likely to evolve in two particular directions:
→ The growth of automation (including 3-D modelling) of the manufacturing process, which will make customisation and irregularly shaped panels less costly
→ A drive toward reduction in energy consumption, both in terms of embodied energy and performance in use.

The latter could be enforced via future revisions of the Building Regulations, which may include a requirement for zero carbon emission buildings.

Changes may include an increased use of:
→ Shading devices or external moveable shutters, as used in continental Europe
→ Opening windows within the building envelope, to provide a 'mixed mode' option, enabling a change to natural ventilation in the future
→ Exposed thermal mass, for example, in the form of concrete panels
→ Fully or partially recycled materials or materials from sustainable resources, for example, timber.

It is likely that documents such as the Code for Sustainable Homes may be adapted for the commercial sector, which could mean that aluminium framing systems will have to be largely substituted by alternative materials or for thermal break technology to further evolve.

The development of lighting technology together with architectural or client driven desires to 'brand' buildings has led to the design of 'Media Façades'. These façades incorporate light-emitting diodes (LEDs) to enable illumination, decoration and messaging, including the display of moving images. Although not yet common, the reduction in cost for LEDs may increase demand for such façades.

The commercial viability of photovoltaic (PV) cells may improve. Combining increased efficiency and the penalty of increasing energy costs, PVs may become a more commercially viable solution for building envelope design. This trend may be supported by legislation, similar to that in Germany, which compels energy providers to buy site-produced energy at a premium rate.

ONE NEW CHANGE DEVELOPMENT
Courtesy of Miller Hare

6.0 /

ENGINE

This section presents the essential criteria for structural loadings, functional criteria, comfort criteria and requirements for building services systems. It also gives a brief overview of requirements for integrating services and structure.

ERING

TALKING POINTS

Sustainability

Business performance

Cost & value

6.0 /

6.1

STRUCTURAL SYSTEMS

The choice of the structural system for a building can be complex. It will be influenced by many factors including site location and site constraints, building form, planning and structural grids, loading requirements, construction budget, occupier flexibility and issues of sustainability.

6.1.1

£ Demountable and moveable partitions can qualify as plant assets for Capital Allowances purposes, subject to a business use test.

£ A reduction in magnitude of the live load will result in savings in the volume of construction materials of the frame and its foundations and, consequently, a saving in the cost of the structural frame.

LOADINGS

Standard allowances for live load
General area: A minimum of 2.5 kN/m² for floors above ground floor and 3.0 kN/m² at, or below, ground floor over approximately 95% of each potentially sub-lettable floor area (source: the NAD to BS EN 1991-1-1:2002)

High loading area
A loading of 7.5 kN/m² over approximately 5% of each potentially sub-lettable floor area and not in primary circulation routes

Historically, UK office buildings have been designed and marketed with live loadings significantly higher than the British Standard loading threshold of 2.5 kN/m² (typically 3.5–4.0 kN/m²). Research has shown this to be an over provision. (Source: Structural floor loading and raised floor specification for office buildings: Stanhope Position Paper, January 2004.)

Standard allowances for dead load
Demountable partitions: 0.5–1.2 kN/m² depending on the self-weight of the partition used (source: BS EN 1991-1-1:2002). Where the partition material is not known, a load of 1.0 kN/m² should be used

Raised floors, ceiling and building services equipment: 0.85 kN/m²

The specification of a reduced but appropriate live load contributes to savings in the volumes of materials in the frame and its foundations – and a reduced impact on the environment.

However, this must be weighted against the fact that an increase in live load may increase the future flexibility and adaptability of the building and thereby potentially increase the life of the building.

The brief and specification for live loading will influence the capacity of areas of the building (or the entire building for that matter) to adapt to a change in use from office to, for example, an auditorium, a restaurant or residential.

The preparation of loading plans to illustrate the specification for the dead and live loads (for inclusion in the record drawing set) will be useful in understanding the assumptions made in the original design when considering a change of use of the building or reuse of the foundations in the future.

The specification of a higher live load than the minimum requirement in general areas can increase the flexibility of the building to accommodate changes in space planning.

The specification of a live load of 7.5 kN/m^2 over 5% of the floor area improves the flexibility of the building to accommodate local storage areas.

6.1.2

FRAME AND MATERIALS

For both low and high-rise office buildings, a steel or concrete structure is equally acceptable. The concrete may be conventionally reinforced or predominantly post-tensioned. Steel and concrete structures are compared in the diagram overleaf. It is not unusual for steel and reinforced concrete elements to combine in a single structural frame.

Timber is also a suitable structural frame material, particularly for low rise office buildings (two to four floors). Timber is particularly suitable for floor structures, either as floor slab systems or as primary beams.

Steel	Concrete
→ Relatively lightweight	→ Relatively heavy
→ Greater depths	→ Shallower depths
→ Minimum depth solutions inefficient	→ For modest spans, reinforced flat slabs give minimum depths.
→ Good for longer spans but depth requirements imply combined structure and services zone	→ Can be efficient on rectangular and square grids
→ More efficient on rectangular grids than on square grids	→ Holes and fixings can be accommodated but strategy must be considered early. Holes should avoid pre-stressing tensions.
→ Inherently good for holes and fixings (into soffit)	→ Mass provides good inherent response to footfall vibration
→ Framing of holes and openings straightforward	→ Fire protection is inherent. No need for intumescent paints which can be harmful to the environment
→ Depth and weight may be governed by footfall dynamics	→ Exposed concrete soffits can allow the omission of ceilings and improve the thermal performance of the building
→ Fire protection is an additional trade	

FURTHER READING
Tall Buildings – A Strategic Design Guide,
BCO, September 2005

Timber can be used in combination with other materials – for example, glued, laminated timber beams with concrete slabs can be used to provide composite floors, or timber floors with steel or concrete columns and cores. Column grids will typically be slightly smaller than those for steel or concrete frames, but floor plates/ spans of 12–15 m are readily achievable. Timber building elements readily lend themselves to prefabrication and speedy erection. Timber structure is possible, and if it is acquired from a renewable source, can reduce the overall environmental impact of the development. This can also be combined with concrete to provide thermal mass.

The increased use of forests and wood products makes an important contribution towards tackling the problem of climate change. Almost 50% of the world's certified forests are found in the EU. Therefore, within the European market, most timber product categories have strong sustainability credentials.

A clear strategy for the sustainable use of structural materials should be developed.

The prefabrication of components of the structure can improve the quality of those components and reduce waste of their constituent materials.

Engineers and contractors set out to standardise details including the sizes of beams and columns, thus producing the most economic solution taking into account the requirements of other disciplines.

Floor slabs may be used for thermal cooling in either steel or concrete framed structures. If the structural soffit is considered unattractive then perforated ceilings can be provided.

The Green Guide to Specification (BRE 2008) can be used to identify materials with the lowest embodied carbon impact. Wherever feasible to use, timber structures often provide the most sustainable solution. However, the use of cement replacement and recycled/secondary aggregates in concrete mixes can significantly reduce the embodied carbon of concrete.

Incorporating recycled materials such as ground granulated blast furnace slag (GGBFS) into concrete can help to reduce the carbon emissions and overall embodied energy of the building.

The relative costs of steel and concrete solutions vary with building form and shape. The cost comparison is influenced by foundation costs (reduced for a lighter steel frame) and construction programme. On the other hand, cost is just one of several considerations in the selection of any scheme and cost comparison between steel and concrete has to be carried out on a project by project basis at an early stage of the design development process.

6.0 /

FLEXIBILITY AND FUTURE ADAPTABILITY

The building structure must also stabilise the building. The stability of the structure can have a major influence on the design, and frequently utilises structural walls located within and around the service cores. Cores are increasingly constructed using slip forming techniques, which means that the core must be shaped to allow it to free stand prior to construction of the floors. These requirements necessitate careful co-ordination of the design.

A clear strategy for flexibility and future adaptability of the structure should be developed. Flexibility should be considered during three phases:

→ Design: Select geometry and performance criteria with flexibility in mind.
→ Construction: Fit-out design may be concurrent with shell and core construction and the design should be able to adapt quickly to minor changes (abnormal loads, additional risers, small holes and fixings).
→ Operation: Modifications are likely to be minor, but it must be possible to form a larger hole. This may be a reasonably complex operation, but it will be an infrequent event (say once in every 20 years).

Future adaptability should be considered, for example new (service) openings, staircases, lifts, extended service risers and infill of any atria.

6.1.4

DEFLECTIONS AND TOLERANCES

The overall dimension of structural zones – and all non-structural elements and finishes connected or applied to the building frame – should be detailed to accommodate:

→ Dead load deflections
→ Setting out and constructional tolerances for the building structure
→ Building frame deflections due to design criteria.

A clear set of interface requirements between the structure and those connecting elements which require specific movement or tolerance criteria should be identified. These are likely to cover such elements as:

→ Lift equipment
→ Building maintenance units (BMUs) such as cleaning cradles or moving gantries
→ Envelope/cladding.

To reduce the deflection of any structural element of a frame, whether it is in steel or concrete, its stiffness/rigidity has to be enhanced. This will result in strengthening of the section, increasing the size or weight of the construction material, and hence increasing its cost.

MONSOON HQ, NOTTING HILL VILLAGE
Photographer: Timothy Soar

6.0 /

6.1.5

FURTHER READING
*Design of Floors for
Vibration: A New
Approach (P354),*
Steel Construction
Institute 2007

*A Design Guide for
Footfall Induced
Vibration of Structures,*
Concrete Society 2006

VIBRATION

The structure of a building can be subjected to a number of actions that can result in vibration. The primary effect tends to be the footfall-induced vibration of floors. However, secondary effects, such as the structural-borne vibration arising from the proximity of a railway, can also be pertinent. Acceptance criteria are often subjective and will depend on the type and quality of office space being considered.

Footfall-induced vibration tends to be significant in lightweight, medium and long span floors. Particular care should be given to the performance criteria of dealer floors and other buildings with sensitive uses.

The effects of vibration may be mitigated by stiffening the floor, increasing mass or damping or, in the case of structural borne vibration, by isolation of the affected areas.

Structural slab vibration due to footfall impacts, plant items, lifts and escalators should be reviewed to ensure mid-span excitation is such that 'adverse comment is not expected' when assessed in accordance with BS 6472-1: 2008 Table 1, based on heavy trafficked floors with nominal live loads (i.e. as in electronic/paperless offices).

6.1.6

FURTHER READING
BCO Security Guide
2009

ROBUSTNESS

The partial collapse of a block of flats at Ronan Point in 1968 was disproportionate to the event that caused it. This led to an amendment of the Building Regulations in 1970 to ensure that a degree of robustness was provided in buildings over five storeys in height. The principal requirement is the provision of effective vertical and horizontal ties so that alternate load paths may be mobilised in the event that the structure is damaged.

The Building Regulations were further amended in 2004 so that, in addition to the existing provisions, many offices will be required to be designed for all abnormal hazards that may be reasonably foreseen during the life of the building.

These hazards are to be identified by a systematic risk assessment and may include, for example, vehicular impact or terrorist attacks.

BISHOPSGATE, LONDON
Copyright: British Land

6.0 /

6.1.7

The refurbishment of an existing building has to be weighed against building a new office building, which may be better suited to modern requirements.

SUSTAINABILITY

Structural-related issues that currently award BREEAM credits include: the use of materials with a low embodied energy, the re-use of existing structures and/or façades, the use of recycled/secondary aggregates and the use of materials that are responsibly sourced.

Key issues to consider in terms of sustainability when deciding on structural system include:

→ **Resource efficiency:** Reduce the amount of new materials through efficient design and the amount of waste during construction/operation by using prefabrication and efficient waste management. Reuse or refurbish existing buildings, or reuse materials in new buildings. Use recycled materials (e.g. for concrete structures maximise the amount of cement replacement and/or recycled/secondary aggregates). Build for deconstruction to enable easy recovery of materials.

→ **Embodied energy:** The embodied energy of a material is the energy used in its processing and transport to site (see Section 4.2.1), often measured through an environmental profiling system such as the *Green Guide for Specification* (BRE 2008). This is aimed at allowing materials to be selected with as low an embodied impact as possible. The use of materials with a low embodied impact will also contribute towards credits under BREEAM.

→ **Operational energy:** The structure is typically not used as part of the active cooling system for a building, but there are ways that it can be. These include utilising the inherent thermal mass of the building (see below) and the use of energy piles.

→ **Thermal mass:** Standard low mass design (ceiling finishes, services distribution, and lighting) has to be weighed against the use of thermal mass, i.e. exposed slabs, which can save on operational energy/carbon, but may carry more embodied energy. Note: It is often not necessary to increase the concrete depth of slabs as in the vast majority of cases there is sufficient mass in even the slimmest of concrete-on-metal-deck slabs. The important issue is to expose the slab in order to enable the slab to absorb/emit heat.

→ Climate change: Climate change may influence the structure via increased wind loads, temperature movements and the requirement to accommodate increased risks of flooding. Water systems for capture or attenuation are being used more frequently and this influences support systems, especially roof structures. The structure also increasingly has to accommodate on-site renewable energy generation systems such as photovoltaics, large biomass boilers, or other loadings such as green roofs.

→ Flexibility: Lean design (lower loadings, minimum weight design) has to be balanced against flexibility when accommodating future requirements, including potential change of use (with possibly higher load requirements).

→ Durability: Designing for long life and future flexibility (the use of durable materials and a solid structure) has to be weighted against designing for a short life and single use (embracing the temporary, use of lightweight materials).

6.1.8

STRUCTURAL FIRE RATING

To comply with Building Regulations and statutory legislation, the fire protection systems and compartmentation requirements for a building must be considered. (See Appendix A2: Statutory regulations)

The building structure can be protected inherently (for example, through element size and cover to reinforcement for reinforced concrete), or by applied finishes, such as paint systems for structural steelwork. Fire engineering approaches can be used in some cases to reduce the statutory requirements and are subject to approval by the appropriate authorities.

6.1.9

HEALTH AND SAFETY

Due attention should be given to health and safety through all aspects and stages of the structural design process and as required by the Construction (Design and Management) Regulations 2007. (See Appendix A3: Health and safety)

NO.8 FITZROY STREET, LONDON
Copyright: Arup/Hufton + Crowe

6.2

BUILDING SERVICES ENGINEERING

The scope of provision for occupiers varies from project to project and developer to developer. The more the provision, the more attractive the building may be to prospective occupiers but the greater the cost of the development. If there is no provision in a scheme, then the developer must ensure that additional installations can be accommodated with minimal disruption to existing occupiers and at an acceptable cost. Equally, developers do not want to invest capital for services that may not be required by the prospective occupier, therefore a balance must be sought.

6.2.1

FUNCTIONAL CRITERIA

Occupancy criteria
Occupancy can be considered in two ways – workplace density and effective density – and these are considered in more detail in Section 3.2. In relation to building services systems, core system design is based on effective density and services related to individual office space should be considered in relation to workplace density.

An occupation density of 12 m^2 per person is used for core design elements such as lifts, toilet provision and water storage calculations

An occupation density of 10 m^2 per person is used for terminal cooling load and outdoor air allowance

Zoning
Office spaces should be zoned in order to provide fit-out flexibility. Any air-conditioning system should allow formation of perimeter and central zones, each with their own independent control of temperature.

6.0 /

The often non-uniform distribution of load across a floor (or number of floors) caused by additional spot loads such as printers, tea points or high density of occupation, means that the distribution system should be able to deliver 25 W/m².

Where a development is being designed to accommodate an occupier that has a trading operation this should be included in the base build design. Typically, the dealer area should allow for: a small power and cooling allowance of 80–100 W/m²; a floor void of ⩾300mm; a floor-to-ceiling height of 3.0m or more; good sight lines across the area; enhanced allowance for floor loading (especially in the main equipment room (MER)); enhanced fresh air allowance; and enhanced occupant density for toilet and water storage. (MER requirements and allowances are given in Section 6.2.7).

Perimeter control zones should typically be no more than 6 m wide and 4.5 m deep. It should be possible to add further terminal units at 3 m intervals where high levels of cellularisation are envisaged without major disruption to the base building installations. This needs careful consideration of the location of terminal units and provision of spare connections on distribution systems.

Internal zones are not subject to solar gains and can be larger, in the range of 50 to 70 m², depending on the choice of system.

Where alternative air-conditioning systems (such as under-floor supply and displacement) are utilised, it should be accepted that perimeter control zones will be much larger. Such systems are better suited to an open plan arrangement with local adaptations made for small meeting rooms and cellular offices.

Building services equipment in the floor or ceiling voids should follow the planning grid to simplify installation of partitions and to avoid unnecessary reconfiguration.

Small power
Small power is the load allowance available for office equipment.

An allowance of 25 W/m² should be used to calculate electrical capacity and cooling loads for the building.

Small power distribution on office floors should be sized for 25 W/m² of the net internal floor area. However, when diversified over an area of 1000 m² or more, power consumption in offices rarely exceeds 15 W/m² and this should be reflected in the assessment of the overall building demand.

Generally, the load increases as the occupation density increases. A typical desk load is 150 W, which equates to 15 W/m² at a workplace density of 1 person per 10 m². The 25 W/m² design figure allows for a reasonable margin of future flexibility and uneven distribution of the load between floors and over floorplates.

FURTHER READING
See *BCO Fit out Guide* for guidance on occupier-specific load requirements

When designing the infrastructure, additional power should be allowed for non-desk loads such as data centres, communication hubs, kitchens and so on. In technology intensive areas such as dealer rooms, calculations should be based on actual or estimated equipment loads.

Small power distribution boards should be provided with a minimum of 25% spare ways. Some provision should also be made for spare sections in the central main switchgear panels and for spare space to allow expansion in the future.

Cooling loads

Solar gains vary with façade orientation and should preferably fall in the range of 50–65 W/m² of the 4.5 m deep perimeter zone. BREEAM encourages anti-glare blinds to be provided as part of the base building and these should be taken into account when assessing comfort conditions.

Occupancy allowances should be made based upon standard floor occupancy of 10 m² per person, unless specific provision is being made to accommodate a known higher occupation density.

Small power cooling loads should match the small power allowance, generally 25 W/m² in the distribution risers and terminal units, to allow occupiers flexibility to deal with 'hot spots', special use areas, and local increased occupation density. The small power cooling load may be diversified at the central plant to allow for a small power consumption of 15 W/m² across the building net area, where a similar provision has been made for the small power load.

The cooling load created by artificial lighting should be designed for no more than 12 W/m², including an allowance for occupier's fit-out installations.

6.0 /

£ £ Increasing resilience
involves increasing costs
and plant space. The level of
resilience demanded by occupiers
will depend on their business need.
Financial services sector occupiers
have a need to meet resilience
levels prescribed by the insurance
industry, and these are detailed
in the tier certification guidance
document published by the
Uptime Institute.

Where possible, space should be allocated for an occupier to install additional cooling plant and heat rejection equipment to deal with 24-hour loads and critical cooling for computer rooms, dealer rooms, and the like. Typically, this could be between 5% and 10% of base building central plant space provision of which 50% should be external space.

Resilience
Resilience describes the ability of a system to continue working during failure or maintenance. It may cover central plant and distribution networks. A general-purpose office building would generally have a single incoming power supply, potentially two boilers and chillers to give partial operation if one unit were to fail, run and standby pumps, but little or no duplication of distribution networks (all dependent on user profile).

More resilience may be provided by:
→ Including standby components (e.g. pumps, boilers, chillers, etc.) in central plant
→ Providing duplicate distribution routes to allow continued operation if one path fails
→ Providing duplicate supplies to the building from the mains, installing standby generators, and avoiding breaks in supply by using uninterruptible power supplies
→ Allocating space for later installation of additional plant by the occupier.

FURTHER READING
Tier Certification Guide,
Uptime Institute

Water
Water is a resource that is likely to become scarcer as climate change has more effect. To minimise water usage, consider: passive infra-red (PIR) control with sequenced flushing of urinals; flow restricted taps for each hand basin with infrared control; low volume and dual-flush WCs; rainwater harvesting; and grey water collection.

Water storage is no longer a statutory requirement for commercial offices. However, water storage is frequently specified to allow continued occupation if the mains water supply fails. Water storage should not exceed 15 litres per person per day, using a diversified building occupancy density of 1 person per 12 m² net area to ensure that the water is 'turned over' frequently to reduce the risk of legionnaires' disease.

Where restaurants and kitchens are anticipated, the base building storage should be increased by 5 litres per person per day (assuming 60% of the building population use the facility).

Water storage for mechanical cooling systems (cooling towers) should provide a minimum of 4 hours running at peak load. This requirement may be significantly increased for business critical cooling systems.

Rainwater may be 'harvested' in a tank for later reuse such as flushing toilets, landscape irrigation, or façade cleaning. Depending on the use, some treatment of the water may be needed.

Rainfall is becoming more intense because of climate change so surface water discharge may have to be attenuated to prevent overloading the sewers:

→ Rainfall intensity design criteria have been increasing as a result of climate change and are likely to continue to increase. Roof areas should be designed in accordance with the data in BS EN 12056-3, using statistical rainfall intensities when available.
→ Hard landscape encourages rapid run-off and options such as porous paving or sustainable urban drainage systems (SUDS) should be considered. Attenuation of run-off may also be achieved by using storage tanks or 'green' roofs that slow down the passage of rainwater.

Greywater is waste water generated by domestic processes such as hand washing, bathing and dishwashing which is collected and recycled to feed non-potable uses. A separate drainage pipework system is needed to prevent contamination by soil waste. Greywater is generally subject to some filtration and disinfection before being pumped through a dedicated distribution pipe network to toilets, planting, etc.

6.0 /

Fit-out and future-proofing

Distribution routes, plant space and structural soft spots should be allowed in order to accommodate additional plant as part of the fitting out works. Provisions should typically include for:

→ Supplementary cooling plant, e.g. for computer rooms and other high density loads
→ Supplementary ventilation plant, e.g. for conference rooms, meeting rooms, kitchens, and so on
→ Satellite equipment, e.g. space for dishes and equipment
→ Tea point facilities with associated water drainage and extract ventilation provisions
→ Standby generation and uninterrupted power supply (UPS), e.g. for critical loads such as computer rooms
→ Kitchen services, e.g. supply and exhaust ventilation, additional water storage of 5 litres per person per day, drainage, water services, power, gas and so on
→ Risers for additional pipe work, cables, etc., e.g. additional cooling, data cabling and the like
→ Extended WC provision.

In large developments where multiple entrances may be formed, supplementary lifts and escalators may be considered.

A strategy for accommodating future occupiers' plant requirements should be clearly set out in the base building design documents. Such a strategy may include reserved space or the conversion of other areas such as storage or car parking areas. Access for future installation and maintenance of occupier's plant through another's demise should be avoided.

Vertical riser space should be incorporated into the core design and should be dedicated for occupiers use. These risers should connect each floor to a minimum of one central plant location.

Financial services sector occupiers may have very demanding plant requirements for computer rooms, additional cooling, and standby power, and it would be unreasonable to try and design for these in all speculative developments.

6.2.2

COMFORT CRITERIA

Internal temperature
A summer air temperature of 24°C should be achieved in an air-conditioned office space

Recent research commissioned jointly by the BCO, RIBA and CoreNet concludes that 24°C provides good comfort and productivity conditions for office occupants and allows a reduction in energy consumption.

Where the system type allows, the winter temperature may be reduced to no less than 20°C to reduce heating energy needs

If there are year-round cooling loads then a reduction in space temperature during winter may cause increased energy consumption. In this case, the winter temperature should be the same as the summer temperature.

A deviation of ±2°C should be allowed for control and operational tolerance

Low energy solutions like displacement and underfloor systems may not achieve this tolerance because they operate on an average temperature across the workspace.

Warmth lowers arousal, exacerbates the symptoms of sick building syndrome, and has a negative effect on mental work. Cold conditions tighten the muscles and so are detrimental to manual dexterity.

A rule of thumb described in the Federation of European HVAC Associations (REHVA) Guidebook number 6 is that every increase in temperature of 1°C above 25°C results in a fall-off in productivity of 2%.

FURTHER READING
CIBSE Guide A:
Environmental design,
CIBSE 2006

CIBSE TM36: Climate
change and the indoor
environment: impacts
and adaptation, CIBSE
2005

6.0 /

An objective measure for thermal comfort can be defined in terms of minimum percentage of people dissatisfied (PPD) using ISO 7730. A Predicted Mean Vote (PMV) of 0 to -0.5 and a Percentage People Dissatisfied (PPD) of no more than 10% should be achieved, and meeting these limits will ensure that occupants will remain comfortable even in more testing areas, e.g. adjacent to highly glazed façades.

Dynamic thermal modelling software is needed to check these comfort conditions and is a prerequisite for a BREEAM assessment. BREEAM encourages anti-glare blinds to be provided as part of the base building and these should be taken into account when assessing comfort conditions.

For mixed mode and naturally ventilated offices, the internal temperature should not exceed 25°C for more than 5% of the occupied hours and 28°C for no more than 1%

Wherever possible the combined effect of the air temperature, radiant temperature and air movement, known as 'operative temperature', should be limited to 26–27°C, which may limit the amount of glazing in the façade.

External temperature will be selected to suit the geographic location. However, predictions of climate change (see www.ukcip.org.uk Climate Change Scenarios) suggest that external summertime temperatures will continue to rise. This should be taken into account for the lifetime of the building fabric when assessing natural ventilation solutions and for the lifetime of the engineering plant when assessing air-conditioning.

Outdoor air is required for respiration and to prevent build up of odours. An allowance of 1.2–1.6 l/s per m^2 should be made, which equates to 12–16 l/s per person based on the standard 1 person per 10 m^2 occupancy density

Where the lower figure is used, it is recommended that at least 10% additional air is allowed to account for meeting rooms and areas of high occupation density.

Table 6.1 Outdoor air rates for differing occupancy densities

Outdoor air rate (l/s per m²)	Floor occupancy density				
	10 m² per person	9 m² per person	8 m² per person	7 m² per person	6 m² per person
1.2	12 l/s per person NOTE NO SPARE	10.8 l/s per person			
1.4	>12 l/s per person SPARE AVAILABLE	>12 l/s per person SPARE AVAILABLE	11.2 l/s per person	<10 l/s per person	
1.6	>12 l/s per person SPARE AVAILABLE	>12 l/s per person SPARE AVAILABLE	>12 l/s per person SPARE AVAILABLE	11.2 l/s per person	

The BCO recommendation: An enhanced fresh air allowance with spare capacity for meeting rooms.
Below the BCO recommended minimum outdoor air allowance per person
Below the statutory outdoor air allowance where additional plant will be required.

Outside air is difficult to add to a building after completion, especially when the building is occupied. Table 6.1 illustrates the implications of different outdoor air rates for differing occupancy densities.

An outdoor air allowance of 1.6 l/s per m^2 facilitates use of a wide range of air-conditioning solutions, including chilled beams. It should be noted that increasing the fresh air delivered to the space will increase the amount of fan energy used by the building but will also increase the amount of potential 'free' cooling delivered to the space.

FURTHER READING
BREEAM for Offices
BRE 2008
CIBSE TM21:
Minimising pollution
at air intakes,
CIBSE 1999

The quality of the outside air is vital to the internal environment and the location of air intakes should be carefully selected to consider potential sources of pollution. Wherever possible, air intakes should be located at least 10 m above ground level to provide some protection against extreme events. In addition, intakes and exhaust points should be separated by at least 10 m and, wherever possible, located 20 m or more from other sources of pollution such as boiler flues, car park vents, roads, etc. Carbon dioxide levels need to be maintained below 1000 ppm.

Air quality, noise and security are issues in dense urban environments, but there may be opportunities in rural or business park environments to use lower level intakes and natural ventilation. Outdoor air should be filtered to a minimum EU7 standard.

30 ST MARY AXE, SWISS RE HEADQUARTERS
Copyright: Foster + Partners. Photographer: Nigel Young

Humidity control should not normally be provided unless special design conditions apply, for instance, very high levels of fresh air. If essential, room humidity should be no less than 35–40% RH. Space should be allowed in air handling plant together with additional gas or electric capacity for later installation of evaporative steam-based systems.

Daylighting

The best lighting for the workplace is daylight. It is the highest quality light, it varies naturally during the day, gives excellent colour rendering and provides the most natural modelling. It is the most 'sustainable' way of providing light to the workplace.

Unless an activity requires the exclusion of daylight, the target should be to provide a view out-of-doors irrespective of its quality. However, although daylight and sunlight have positive qualities they must be carefully controlled to avoid glare. Legal requirements for the control of glare are within the Health and Safety (Display Screen Equipment) Regulations 1992.

In order for the BREEAM credit for 'glare control' to be awarded, the glare control blinds should be installed as part of the base building.

An occupant's visual perception of a space is related to the brightness of the visible surfaces. Good daylight and carefully controlled sunlight can greatly enhance the appearance of a space.

Target daylighting: an average daylight factor of 2% or more; uniformity ratio, of at least 0.4 or a minimum point daylight factor of at least 0.8%

Optimum standards for office workplace are for at least 80% of net lettable office floor area to be adequately daylit. Where deeper plan buildings are unavoidable atria should be strategically located to provide a view of a daylit space.

FURTHER READING
CIBSE Lighting Guide 10 Daylighting and window design, CIBSE 1999

BS 8206 Lighting for buildings Part 2. Code of practice for daylighting, BSI 1992

FURTHER READING
BS EN 15193: Energy performance of buildings – Energy requirements for lighting, BSI 2007

The Health and Safety (Display Screen Equipment) Regulations 1992: United Kingdom CIBSE Lighting Guide LG10: Daylight and window design, CIBSE 1999

6.0 / ENGINEERING

THREADNEEDLE STREET, LONDON
Copyright: Hammerson

Artificial lighting

Artificial lighting is a key element in ensuring a healthy and productive working environment. It has to satisfy the requirements of a wide range of workplace tasks undertaken by a large diversity of people with different needs and wants.

Artificial lighting levels for offices should be in the range of 300–500 lux. However, the illumination level is only the starting point in defining a successful office lighting installation. Further guidance is given in Section 6.2.4 and the forthcoming *BCO Office Lighting Guide*. The *BCO Office Lighting Guide* will be a source of in-depth guidance and information on how to create exciting and sustainable lighting solutions to meet the BCO criteria.

Ventilation and comfort control systems

There are many types of comfort control systems available, each having its own performance characteristics and being suited to different applications. The factors that affect choice of system include:

→ Magnitude of cooling loads
→ Space requirements
→ Flexibility to accommodate change
→ Capital cost
→ Controllability
→ Maintenance and life cycle costs
→ Energy consumption.

The selection of an appropriate comfort control system is key to the acceptability of the internal environment, the building's energy performance certificate (EPC) rating, and the energy consumed by the building.

£₤ The choice of air-conditioning system (if required) will depend on a number of factors. Any one of these factors may have a corresponding effect on cost and value; therefore each development should be assessed in isolation.

FURTHER READING
*CIBSE Guide B:
Heating, Ventilation,
Air Conditioning and
Refrigeration,*
CIBSE 2005

*BCO Fit out Guide:
Engineering System
Strategy and Design,*

Heating, ventilation and air conditioning installations, and hot and cold water systems are eligible for tax relief. 100% tax relief is available for energy saving technologies qualifying under the Enhanced Capital Allowances (ECA) scheme.

Appropriate systems for office developments are:
→ Fan coil units (where possible using DC drive fan motor technology)
→ Variable refrigerant volume or flow (VRV/VRF)
→ Passive or active chilled beams
→ Chilled ceilings
→ Under floor or displacement systems
→ Variable air volume (VAV)
→ Natural or mixed mode ventilation.

Whichever system is selected, designs should exploit natural or waste energy. Energy recovery and 'free cooling' should be used in central plant wherever feasible and connection to district or community energy systems considered where they are available.

The choice of system needs to be considered in conjunction with the application of any low and zero carbon (LZC) technologies, which need to be fully integrated into the engineering system design to maximise the potential benefit.

Appendix A8: Options for controlling the indoor environment, presents a general comparison of the advantages and disadvantages of the various office air-conditioning systems commonly used in the UK.

Providing individual or limited 'local' control can improve the building occupants' perception of their workspace. While it is not always possible to provide this control, particularly for HVAC and lighting in an open plan office, some sort of individual control should be considered by the design and/or fit-out team.

Automatic controls for comfort

Automatic controls should: govern temperatures and times of operation of air-conditioning; allow part-floor operation where there are large floor plates; and monitor performance of systems to provide alarms and feedback on performance. An optional enhancement may be provided for occupants to make limited adjustments to the heating and air-conditioning systems and receive notification of alarms from the base building plant to alert them to conditions that might affect their business.

Research shows that occupants perceive higher levels of comfort in buildings that have simple, accessible controls. Well-maintained and managed building services are also rated higher by users than are poorly maintained and managed installations. In general, buildings that give individual occupants greater control over their local conditions are regarded as more comfortable. As an example, naturally ventilated buildings, which are designed to wider temperature bands, tend to be perceived as relatively comfortable because they are both easier to manage and allow more personal control.

In multi-occupier buildings, provision should be made for individual occupiers to request extensions of running periods.

Automatic controls are generally provided in the form of a Building Management System (BMS), which is based on intelligent local controllers at plant items linked to a central PC supervisory terminal via a data network. The BMS should have sufficient capacity to allow integration of the occupier's fit out.

€£ Information
technology systems
qualify for tax relief, unless
these are paid for by
occupiers.

Intelligent buildings

For many years, voice and data systems were provisioned separately. However, it is now becoming common practice to use an integrated and common structured cabling system. Like the voice and data systems of the past, typical construction projects have separately installed each of the building automation system disciplines under different packages of the mechanical or electrical contract. However, depending on the nature of the building occupancy, ownership and management, consideration should be given to the total integration of building technology systems along with audio/visual and information and communications technology (ICT) systems onto one common network platform. Benefits may include a reduction in both installation and whole life costs.

By integrating systems onto a common network the opportunity arises to provide a truly intelligent building allowing seamless integration of different systems. Typically an integrated Building Management System (iBMS) will incorporate:

→ CCTV
→ Access control
→ Intruder alarm
→ Building management system
→ Automatic meter reading system
→ Lighting controls
→ Lift monitoring system
→ Display screens/touch screens
→ Power control systems
→ Electronic building records
→ Planned preventative maintenance systems
→ Asset management systems
→ Management reporting
→ Voice and data.

FURTHER READING
CIBSE Guide H:
Building Control
Systems, CIBSE 2000

Specifying Building
Management Systems,
BSRIA 1998

Standard Specification
for BMS, BSRIA 2001

Other interfaces may be formed with fire and life safety systems. but these are usually operated over separate networks.

Access to the BMS and automatic meter reading systems also allows for real-time monitoring and display of energy use and associated carbon emissions. This information may be displayed in a building entrance or on a freely accessible web page to allow occupants to see and understand how much energy they are using.

This approach provides a level of future proofing because equipment and appliances are being developed to follow industry standard IP-based protocols heading towards a 'plug and play' solution for adding to existing systems.

An iBMS will require an equipment room and wiring concentration points. The iBMS equipment room will house the landlord's incoming telecommunications, the iBMS and associated system servers, CCTV storage and iBMS network hardware.

The room should be located centrally, with good distribution access to cores and risers and away from electrical sub-stations and switchgear. The room should be secure, ventilated, environmentally controlled, with resilient uninterruptible power supplies and automatic fire extinguishing equipment. The iBMS Equipment Room should be adjacent to the central control and security room, if there is one.

Typical provisions required for the iBMS Equipment Room are similar to those described for the building Main Equipment Room (MER) (see Section 6.2.7 for details) but on a smaller scale.

ELECTRICAL SYSTEMS

Incoming power supplies

Depending on the size of the building, the incoming electrical supply may be provided at either high voltage or low voltage. New buildings with an electrical load in excess of 1.0 MVA will generally require a high voltage (HV) supply.

Whatever the type of supply, utility intake rooms will be needed. The number of rooms, their size, ventilation needs, and access provisions will vary and should be agreed at an early stage with the utility provider.

Several different supply configurations are commonly available from utility providers, each offering different levels of resilience. It is important to decide the degree of resilience at the start of a project, taking into account the needs of potential occupiers. Occupiers with business-critical facilities, e.g. financial services companies, are generally the most demanding and often need high standards for protected services, multiple supplies and capacity for enhanced onsite standby power generation.

Building power distribution

Power is distributed vertically through the building in electrical riser shafts, using either cabling or busbar systems.

Individual electrical risers can generally serve between 500 m^2 and 1000 m^2 of office floor area, but this will depend on the depth of the raised floor and the occupation density.

Depending upon the level of resilience appropriate for the building, there should be a minimum of two separate electrical risers with one provided for each potential sub-tenancy on every floor.

The electrical risers should be protected from potential water damage. Piped services should not be installed in the electrical risers.

Standby generation

A strategy should be developed so that occupiers can be allowed to install standby power generation. Ideally, space should be allocated to allow occupiers to install equipment including fuel storage, exhausts and noise and vibration control measures when needed.

Where space is restricted, the developer may choose to provide stand-by generation or to increase the capacity of the life safety set to provide stand-by power for occupiers. The power distribution system should be designed to accommodate the generation strategy.

Renewable and low carbon power generation

The energy strategy, and/or specific occupier requirements, may require some form of embedded low carbon power generation to be provided within the building (for example, CHP/CCHP, fuel cells, wind turbines or photovoltaics).

Where technologies such as wind turbines or photovoltaics are proposed, it is important to consider how their output can best be utilised without the need for batteries. The low carbon power sources should be operated in parallel with the utility supply subject to the approval of the supply authority and the installation of appropriate metering.

Earthing

The earthing installation should be designed and installed in accordance with BS7671 and BS 7430. Multiple earthing connections should be provided to raised floors and false ceilings and connected back to the electrical risers.

Life safety power supplies

Life safety and essential services loads, e.g. sprinkler pumps, wet riser pumps, fire fighting lifts, evacuation lifts, stair pressurisation, and smoke extract systems, need to be provided with dual electrical supplies.

One of these supplies is generally provided by the general power supply from the mains and the other must be from a separate independent source. It may be possible to take an independent power supply from another part of the mains network, but typically a stand-by generator is provided.

6.0 /

ENGINEERING

Since April 2008, electrical installations including general power and lighting are eligible for tax relief as integral features. Lighting including white LED units may qualify for 100% relief under the Enhanced Capital Allowances (ECA) scheme.

The cables carrying power to life safety equipment must have diverse routes and be fire-protected in accordance with the requirements of BS 8491 and the building control authority. The equipment itself must be fed from adjacent automatic changeover devices installed within the same fire compartment.

Lightning protection
The building may require protection against lightning strikes. The risk assessment and design process are laid out in BS EN 62305.

Wherever possible, the design should make use of the building's structural frame, and connections to earth may use the foundations piles. If the structure is used, then it should be tested to prove its suitability. Where the structure cannot be used, down-conductors and earth termination electrodes should be provided.

Power factor correction and harmonic filters
Power factor correction may be used to reduce energy costs and to help comply with Part L of Building Regulations. Also, because many building loads are not linear, e.g. variable speed drives, luminaire ballasts, etc, there is a risk of harmonic distortion. Space should be allocated to allow occupiers to add harmonic filters if their loads require.

Electricity metering
A metering strategy should be developed to meet Part L of the Building Regulations. The meters will be used to monitor energy consumption and help apportion service charges. They will also help to fine tune the building's operation and reduce its carbon emissions. Remote reading of the meters should be considered, via the BMS or iBMS, to allow easy collection of data and automatic analysis of consumption trends.

172

A Metering and Sub-metering timeline to achieve code compliance

	2008	2009	2010
2006 Part L (from April 06)			
Approved Document L2A New non-domestic buildings in England & Wales

TM39:2006 Building Energy Metering (2nd Tier doc supporting ADL2A) | For Buildings over 1000 m², at least 90% of each fuel metered by end-use (heating, lighting, etc) Metering of heating or cooling for each tenancy greater than 2500 m² within building | | Similar for 2010 Part L? |
2008 Display Energy Certificates (from Oct 08)			
DECs for public buildings – offices not affected (yet – see LES-TER below)	For public buildings over 1000 m², at least 95% of the energy used must be accounted for. In the case of site-level metering, energy may be apportioned to a building , or a tenancy, based on floor area.		Government intends to increase these requirements
LES-TER			
BPF voluntary scheme for offices to gather energy data to encourage reduced energy use and cost for both landlord and tenant	In the case of site-level metering, energy may be apportioned to a building, or a tenancy, based on floor area. This voluntary scheme encourages submetering, where appropriate.		DECs extended to cover offices, based on LES-TER method for landlord/tenant split?
Carbon Reduction Commitment			
DEFRA scheme for organisations with electricity consumption greater than 6,000 MWh per annum, who are not already part of the EU emissions scheme	Consultation	Regulations come into force April 2010	Introductory phase (1st capped phase begins 2013)

Courtesy of ES Research & Consultancy

6.0 /

6.2.4

ARTIFICIAL LIGHTING

The visual environment is a significant factor in promoting the productivity and health and safety of office-based staff. There are three principle aspects of lighting that must be balanced in order to provide a visually comfortable working environment:

→ Performance – Light for the performance of the task
→ Ambience – Light to reveal the space, interior design and architecture
→ Comfort – Light to ensure that the task can be carried out comfortably and without strain.

All aspects of office lighting design will be covered in more detail in the *BCO Office Lighting Guide.*

Performance
Performance is about ensuring that there is enough light, in the right place and delivered in a manner that is not uncomfortable for the occupant.

Average maintained illumination levels should be between 300 lux and 500 lux on the working plane

The current BS EN 12464 requires office illumination levels to be 500 lux, which is appropriate for predominantly paper-based tasks. Where work is more usually carried out on a computer screen (VDU) then a level of 300–500 lux is more appropriate.

At the design stage, three main options are available for specifying the average maintained illuminance for the open plan office space: 300 lux, 400 lux or 500 lux. Each of the levels has an impact on the need for an occupier to enhance the base lighting.

Enhancements to raise a local task area to 500 lux for paper-based tasks would normally be provided by the occupier, in the form of desk-mounted task lights (providing the general illumination is above 300 lux). However, if the general illumination level drops below 300 lux – as it may when cellular partitions are installed – then the occupier will need to install additional fixed lighting. A summary of the typical enhancements for each option is shown in the Table 6.2.

£ / £ For most speculative office developments 400 lux average maintained illuminance is the optimum design solution for the landlord and occupier, as efficient lighting schemes can be designed with the minimum need for occupier enhancement.

Table 6.2 Summary of occupier enhancements depending on based design average maintained illuminance

Cat A base design Average maintained illumination	Open plan computer task	Open plan paper based task	Cellular office computer task	Cellular office paper based task
300lux	✓	Additional task lighting required	Additional fixed lighting required	Additional fixed light and task lights required
400lux	✓	Additional task lighting required	✓	Additional task lighting required
500lux	✓	✓	✓	Additional task lighting required

Cat A lighting systems should be dimmable to reduce energy consumption (and therefore cut carbon emissions), negating the need for over-lighting an office area to account for future reduction in light output due to dust, dirt and decreasing lamp output (see Maintenance factor, below). Regardless of which illumination option is selected, the installed lighting should be dimmed to maintain a constant illumination level of 300 lux unless it is known that paper-based tasks will be used (usually at the Cat B fit out).

In all cases the controls and power infrastructure should be provided for additional supplementary and feature lighting to be added to allow the occupier to comply if they wish to with the recommendations given in the Society of Light and Lighting (SLL) *Lighting Guide LG7: Office Lighting*.

Uniformity: BS EN 12464-1 recommends a task area uniformity of 0.7 and an immediate surrounding area / background area uniformity of 0.5 (where uniformity is the ratio of minimum illuminance to average illuminance on a surface). For speculative lighting solutions a target of 0.7 should be achieved.

Where the desk layout is known the lower uniformity figures can be exploited in walkways and break out areas for a more interesting lighting scheme.

Unified Glare Rating (UGR) target should be no greater than 19

Higher figures may be acceptable but more care and attention will be required and a detailed assessment of the office layout will be necessary. A UGR rating of significantly less than 19 (12 and below) may indicate a poorly lit space.

The Health and Safety (display screen equipment) Regulations 1992 require that veiling reflections on screens should be avoided. Guidance on how to achieve this is given in SLL LG7.

→ **Maintenance factor:** This should be no less than 0.8 for office lighting. Low maintenance factors will have an impact on the initial number of lights required to achieve the design average maintained illuminance level.

→ **Colour rendering:** The SLL Code for Lighting set a minimum colour rendering index of Ra → 80 for offices, and only lamps that exhibit this colour rendering index should be used.

→ **Colour temperature:** A lamp colour temperature of Intermediate 3300 – 5300K (Typically 4000K) should be used for the main office lighting. Other colour temperature can be used for feature or display lighting.

Ambience
The Cat A scheme should maximise daylight where possible and use the artificial lighting to ensure that the surfaces within the office are adequately lit (see Luminance distribution, below).

Comfort

Visual comfort can only be achieved by getting the performance and ambience of the lighting design correct. However, there are other contributing factors, including: the luminance balance within the space; the surface finishes; modelling; and level of control.

→ **Luminance balance (illuminance balance) and surface reflectance:** Luminance balance is a key criterion for assessing visual comfort for a lighting installation. The relative brightness of all of the surfaces within field of vision affects how the space is perceived. If the contrast is too high, fatigue may be experienced; too low and a dull and unstimulating environment may result.

For ease of calculation, luminance figures have historically been converted into illuminance ratios. The CIBSE lighting guides (LG 7) recommend that target illuminance levels of 50% and 30% of the task illumination are apparent on the walls and ceilings respectively. This criterion should only be applied to a Cat B lighting design, as it is entirely dependent upon the floor finish, desk layout and type, partitioning, decoration etc. As a target, the Cat A lighting design should aim to achieve as close to The CIBSE LG7 criteria as is reasonably practical with the selected lighting solution.

In undertaking these calculations, the surface brightness of the light fittings may be taken into account. Modern computer programmes provide the facility to undertake a luminance distribution analysis, which will provide a much more accurate assessment of the overall appearance of the space than the crude illuminance method.

Energy use for lighting

In order to assess the amount of energy used, and hence carbon emitted, it is necessary to make an assessment of the energy used by the lighting system over the whole year, with the effects of daylight, occupancy and parasitic loads included. This is achieved by calculating the Lighting Energy Numeric Indicator (LENI), as defined by EN 15193:2007. The LENI figure is expressed as $kWh/m^2/year$.

FURTHER READING
BCO Office Lighting Guide

SLL Code for Lighting, Society of Light and Lighting

CIBSE Lighting Guide 7: Office Lighting, Society of Light and Lighting

BS 12464: *Light and lighting – Lighting of work places – Part 1: Indoor work places,* BSI

Energy usage and lighting controls

The Health and Safety (display screen equipment) Regulations 1992

6.0 /

ENGINEERING

FURTHER READING
BS EN 15193:2007:
*Energy performance
of buildings – Energy
requirements for
lighting*, BSI

*BCO Office Lighting
Guide*

(£)(£) Daylighting will not
save energy unless
lights are switched off when
they are not needed, so
appropriate sensors or
switching controls are needed
to realise energy savings.

(£)(£) Automatic lighting
control systems have
become increasingly
sophisticated, but their
potential energy savings are
frequently not fully achieved.
This is often because the
design philosophy was not
clearly communicated to the
building management staff
and users.

Lighting energy use: The target should be between
15 kWh/m^2/year and 30 kWh/m^2/year

It is recommended that electrical and cooling systems are
provided to cope with a lighting capacity of 12 W/m^2 across the
net internal office area inclusive of the Cat B fit out allowance

Lighting controls

For all but the simplest offices (where it may be deemed
uneconomical), a centralised lighting control system should
be installed to maximise the energy savings from the correct
operation of the lighting system. Self-controlling lights with
integrated daylight and occupancy sensing should only be
used in very small offices where a centralised system cannot
be justified.

Providing daylight in buildings while avoiding glare has
a positive effect on the occupants' perception of the space in
which they work. Studies show that increased daylighting levels
not only make office workers feel more productive, but can
increase retail sales and student test scores. Installing lighting
controls to hold off the lights, either when there is adequate
daylight or when the space is unoccupied, can significantly
reduce the electricity required for lighting.

The principal purpose of the lighting control system is that it
provides an automatic means of only using the right amount
of artificial light, when it is required. The two most important
factors are daylight availability and occupancy. In order to
maximise these factors, for saving energy, the following
should be standard provision for office lighting:

→ Constant illuminance control to dim lights to the desired
   maintained illuminance level
→ Occupancy control via movement and absence detectors
→ Daylight linking via automatic dimming of perimeter lights.

It is common to include additional modes of operation such
as timed scheduling facilities, corridor hold feature and
manual override.

The Cat A lighting control system should provide the infrastructure but not necessarily the installation of sensors and detectors. Sensors, detectors and the commissioning required to operate the constant illuminance control, occupancy control and daylight linking should be provided by the occupier to suit the final office layout.

Emergency lighting

Emergency lighting systems should be designed in accordance with BS 5266, based on either self-contained luminaires complete with 3-hour integral battery packs; or a central battery system.

Automatic self-test and reporting systems should be considered to ensure that the test regimes required by BS 5266 are carried out and that reports of any defects identified by the tests are recorded.

Consideration should be given to the suitability of LED sources, which are beginning to offer a practical alternative to conventional lamps.

BP TRADING OPERATIONS AT 20 CANADA SQUARE, CANARY WHARF, LONDON
Photographer: Richard Waite

179

6.2.5

BMS, control systems, security and alarm systems all qualify for capital allowances.

FURTHER READING
BCO Security Guide,
2009

SAFETY AND SECURITY SYSTEMS

Fire alarm systems

Fire alarm systems should be designed in accordance with BS 5839. A critical part of the design process is to identify the classification of the fire alarm system. This can be established by consultation with the building control authority and the building owner and occupier. This will dictate the level of fire alarm cover to be provided.

A voice alarm system should be installed as part of the fire alarm system when the fire strategy for the building calls for phased evacuation.

Where there is a Code requirement, a fire telephone system should be provided to allow fire-fighters to communicate between the fire control room and the lobbies in the fire fighting shaft.

Wiring for the fire alarm, voice alarm, fire telephone and associated mechanical fire systems must have the correct level of fire resistance. The fire alarm cables should take diverse routes wherever possible to increase resilience.

In multi-occupied buildings, fire alarm systems should allow for individual floors to be isolated, allowing modifications to be made without interrupting operation of the base build system. Large office buildings generally require a Fire Command Centre. The Fire Command Centre is typically at ground floor level adjacent to the fireman's entrance.

Security systems

It is usual for perimeter security systems to be provided as part of the base build, with wireway provision made for the doors that separate an occupier's space from the common areas. The security strategy will generally consider:

→ CCTV to the perimeter and reception area
→ Access control to external entrances and exits and specialist sensitive areas such as security rooms or computer rooms
→ Intruder alarms on external and sensitive doors.

For large and mixed-use schemes such a provision may result in the need for a central security room. The security room should be located in a central position and be provided with resilient UPS power and environmentally controlled conditions.

6.2.6

INFORMATION TECHNOLOGY

Modern offices are highly dependant on IT systems to drive their business functions. The base building design should allow for IT services to enter the building and be easily distributed throughout the building.

Occupiers will need space to install their own business IT systems with all the security and infrastructure requirements that are required to support them.

With the advent of integrated Building Management Systems (iBMS) in large developments (see Section 6.2.2), allowance may be needed for a landlord's IT network to be distributed throughout the building.

Allowance should be made for external duct connections, telecommunication intake rooms, data/telecom risers, occupier equipment rooms, Wi-Fi and satellite services.

External ducts and connections

Consideration should be given to providing geographically diverse intake positions for links to the external telecommunications infrastructure. This will allow occupiers to have multiple connections from one or more of the many telecommunications company networks, increasing the resilience and choice of services. Telecommunications companies seldom share physical duct routes or external access chambers. Multiple intake ducts should be provided for each intake position and space allocated to connect to separate access chambers in the carriageway.

Telecoms intake rooms

Buildings designed to house business-critical operations will require multiple telecommunications intake rooms, with occupiers taking services from more than one provider to increase resilience.

Telecoms companies will share common intake rooms. The intake rooms accommodate the equipment required to convert the external-grade low-smoke zero-halogen (LSOH) cabling to internal grade cabling. Active equipment should be located within landlord or occupier Main Equipment Rooms (MERs) where a controlled environment can be provided.

The telecoms intake rooms should be as close to the intake points as possible at the perimeter of the building. They should preferably be located below or at ground floor level and provide space for several telecommunications companies' equipment in addition to British Telecom. The room should be physically separated, secure, clean, dry, ventilated, well lit and – most importantly – at low risk of flooding. Ideally, other engineering services should run through the telecommunications intake rooms.

Data/telecoms risers

Dedicated containment pathways should be provided from the telecoms intake rooms to dedicated data/telecoms risers. Where business-critical telecommunications services are required, ideally two physically separated data/telecoms risers should be provided, for resilience. Where office floors have the capability of being sub-divided for different occupiers, consideration should be given to providing at least one dedicated data/telecoms riser per tenancy. In multi-occupier buildings, the data/telecoms risers should generally be in the common parts.

Space should be provided in the data/telecoms risers for occupiers to install incoming telecommunications services and IT cabling between floors. In large, multi-occupied buildings, the riser space should be capable of being sectionalised so that areas can be assigned to different occupiers on different floors sharing the same riser. The containment provision should allow adequate space for occupiers to install lockable trunking and for some future growth in occupiers needs over the life of the building.

Where possible data/telecoms risers should not be located adjacent to electrical power risers.

Wireless networks, Wi-Fi

Consideration may be given to providing Wi-Fi access to common parts of the building such as entrance spaces or common break-out areas. Landlord Wi-Fi systems are also being used more commonly for facilities management and building operation services.

Occupiers may wish to install a Wireless Local Area Network (WLAN), which is now commonly used for meeting rooms, break-out spaces and reception areas. Wireless access points are normally installed at high level in the ceiling. Modern wireless access points are rapidly making use of Power over Ethernet (PoE) and becoming less dependent on 230 V local power.

Satellite service

Consideration should be given at roof level for occupiers to install satellite dishes for data communications and television signal reception. In the UK, geo-stationary satellites appear at low elevation angle around 30-degrees above the horizon. The dish location should allow for a clear line of sight from 60-degrees east of south to 60-degrees west of south to ensure that all commonly used business and television satellites are visible.

6.2.7

OCCUPIERS' MAIN EQUIPMENT ROOM (MER)

For large buildings, provision should be made to accommodate the infrastructure requirements that an occupier may need to support a Main Equipment Room (MER), normally within their own demise. (These may occupy up to 3% of the net lettable floor area). This should include:

→ Resilient power supplies – An allowance of 500–2000 W/m^2 (excluding power to specialist cooling systems) may be required to provide resilient power supplies to occupier's computer rooms. The capacity should be included within the incoming electrical supply to support this load, with the ability to allow the occupier to enhance the electrical distribution system to accommodate the requirements. Resilient power may also be provided by the

addition of occupier UPS and standby generation. (Where occupiers need to install their own battery-backed UPS on an office floor, part of the floor area near to the core should have an enhanced load capability.)

→ 24-hour cooling – Plant and riser space will need to be provided for an occupier to install their own equipment.

Occupiers' Secondary or Satellite Equipment Room (SER)
Occupiers may require Secondary or Satellite Equipment Rooms (SER) to distribute copper grade IT cabling. Normally an allowance of one SER per core per floor is sufficient, unless very large floor plates are proposed. Additional power and cooling will be required to accommodate these rooms, and these should be treated in much the same fashion as the MER room provisions but with reduced allowances.

6.3

SERVICES–STRUCTURE INTEGRATION

The overall dimensions for services and structural zones will depend on the frame solution, and extent and type of services provided. For column grids up to 9 m centres, it is usual to keep the horizontal services in a separate zone from the structure, although this should be reviewed for urban buildings where overall height is critical. For longer spans, a different strategy is needed to avoid large storey heights.

The space occupied by long-span beams is generally the main area of services distribution. Structural beams and building services should be integrated in a compact zone, but not so tightly arranged that buildability, access, and flexibility are compromised. Structure–services integration can make substantial savings in storey height, albeit at the expense of more complex structural components and potentially less flexible services solutions.

Where a shell and core only development is undertaken, a notional Category A design should be prepared in sufficient detail to demonstrate that the fit-out can be implemented. Figure 6.1 shows the integration of building services with structure.

→ A suspended ceiling zone may be needed to conceal building services. Where natural ventilation or underfloor air conditioning is used, ceilings may not be needed and exposed soffits may be considered. If lighting is integral with the suspended ceiling system, a zone of 100 mm (including the thickness of the ceiling tile) is commonly used.

A raised floor system of removable tiles on pedestals may be provided to conceal power and data wiring. Typically, a zone of 150 mm (including the thickness of the raised tile) is adequate, although if an underfloor air-conditioning system is used, the overall floor zone may increase to 300–500 mm. Where a floor void is used for air distribution, special care is needed to limit leakage.

If it is expected that the building may incorporate dealing operations or an internet exchange, then the floor zone may be increased to an overall depth of 300–500 mm. Such specialised operations will need enhanced specifications for the flooring system itself to accommodate higher structural loadings.

3 HARDMAN STREET, SPINNINGFIELDS, MANCHESTER
Photographer: David Jewell

7.0 /

VERTIC
TRANS

This section provides best practice advice across
a broad range of vertical transportation issues.
It recognises the recent trend towards increased
occupancy densities and includes guidance on
machine-roomless lifts, energy efficiency,
firefighting lifts, evacuation lifts, ride quality,
tall buildings and escalators.

AL
PORTATION

7.1	LIFTS
7.2	ESCALATORS

TALKING POINTS

Sustainability

Business performance

Cost & value

7.1

£ Lift installations are eligible for capital allowances as an integral feature, including all of the control gear, motors, car and doors. The shaft is usually ineligible, unless it is formed within an existing building.

BREEAM 2008 provides up to two points for energy efficient lift design.

LIFTS

Standards for lift performance need to be specified to reflect the type of lift control system being used. The two most common forms of control used in office buildings are:

→ Conventional control (full collective)
→ Destination control (hall call allocation) where users input their destination floor and are advised which lift will take them to their destination.

This Section presents design criteria and methodologies for destination control and aligns criteria for conventional control using average waiting times rather than average interval times.

Energy efficient lifts should:
→ Operate in a standby mode during off-peak and idle periods (where standby mode is defined as car lights/fans/displays off and traffic control system, drive control and door operator powered down)
→ Use variable voltage, variable frequency drive control
  → Use regenerative lift drives where beneficial
  → Use low-energy lighting sources
  → Be traction lifts (for passenger lifts), rather than hydraulic lifts.

14 CORNHILL, LONDON
Photographer: Cooper Rose

FURTHER READING
CIBSE Guide D:
Transportation systems
in buildings, CIBSE

British Standard
BS 5655 Part 6
Code of practice for
the selection and
installation of new
lifts, BSI

British Standard BS
EN81-70 Accessibility
to lifts for persons
including persons with
disability, BSI

Passenger lifts should generally:

→ Be designed to serve an overall population (effective density) of 1 person per 12 m^2 (net internal area, NIA); this reflects a workplace density of 1 person per 10 m^2 with a utilisation of just over 80%
→ Be selected from a manufacturer's standard range (the use of standard, pre-engineered components reduces capital costs, maintenance costs and the risk of unreliability)
→ Be supplemented by escalators, where appropriate, to accommodate high-density occupancy floors such as financial trading floors at lower levels in the building
→ Be located to offer a choice between lifts and main stairs for both occupants and visitors gaining access to the first few floors; however, no allowance should be made in design calculations unless the stairs are guaranteed to be accessible at all times
→ Be designed to meet the accessibility needs of people using the building
→ Be designed for a minimum lifetime of 15–20 years
→ Have lift car interiors as an integral part of the design of the entrance hall
→ Consider provision of spare cables for future CCTV and access control systems.

133 HOUNDSDITCH, LONDON
Copyright: Sutton Young

7.1.1

CONVENTIONAL CONTROL (FULL COLLECTIVE)

Requirements for passenger lifts operating under conventional control:

Lifts should provide an up-peak handling capacity of 15% of the design population in a five minute period for a single occupancy building. In multi-occupancy buildings, consideration may be given to a slight reduction (12–15%).

Lifts should target an up-peak average waiting time at the main entrance of no more than 25 s with average car loading nominally to no more than 80% of rated capacity. At this car loading, this is broadly equivalent to an average interval between lift departures from the main entrance of no more than 30 s.

Lifts should be analysed for performance during a two-way 'lunchtime' demand where the design up-peak handling capacity of less than 15% has been applied, or in very complex buildings or buildings containing high attraction floors such as restaurants. In these instances the lifts should provide a two-way lunchtime handling capacity of at least 12% of the design population in a five minute period (e.g. 5% up, 2% inter-floor and 5% down) and target a lunchtime average waiting time across all served floor of not more that 40 s, with cars loaded nominally to not more than 80% of rated capacity.

Where scenic lift cars are used, then lower car loading factors should be considered ranging from 70% for partially scenic through to 60% for fully scenic.

7.1.2

DESTINATION CONTROL (HALL CALL ALLOCATION)

Requirements for passenger lifts operating under destination control:

→ Lifts should be designed using simulation software in conjunction with specialist advice. (Figure 7.1 illustrates the typical operation of these lifts.)

Lifts should provide an up-peak handling capacity of at least 15% of the design population in a five minute period.

Lifts should target an up-peak average waiting time at the main entrance of no more than 25 s, with car loading nominally to no more than 80% of rated capacity.

→ Average waiting times of up to 30 s may be acceptable in cases where the average time to destination is 80 s or less.

Lifts should target an up-peak average time to destination from the main entrance of no more than 90 s.

→ Average time to destination of up to 110 s may be acceptable where the average waiting time is less than 25 s.

Lifts should provide a two-way 'lunchtime' handling capacity of at least 12% of the design population in a five minute period (e.g. 5% up, 2% inter-floor and 5% down); and target a 'lunchtime' average waiting time across all served floors of not more than 40 s with cars loaded nominally to not more than 80% of rated capacity.

→ Lifts should be designed so that the destination input panels at the main access levels are located on the approach path to the lobby. Where panels are located remote from the lobby, then additional studies should be carried out to ensure efficient management of the lift control system.

Waiting time does not include walking time from destination input panel to lift lobby. Typically, destination input panels should not be located more than 20 metres from the lift lobby.

4 BROADGATE
Courtesy of ThyssenKrup Elevators UK

Figure 7.1 Destination control - Definition of time to destination (Courtesy of D2E International)

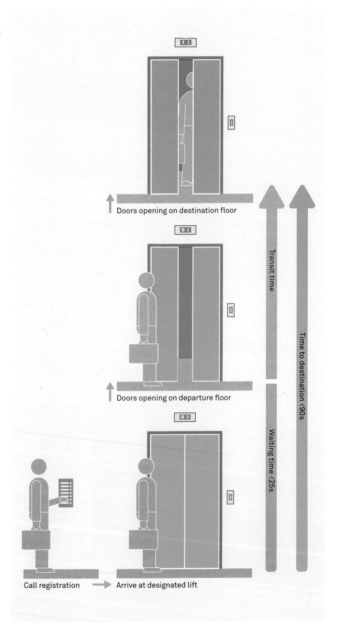

Traffic simulation

Simulation should be used to analyse system performance both in up-peak and lunchtime traffic patterns for destination control lifts. Typical traffic demand templates rise and fall around the specified peak handling capacity. Simulations should be run multiple times and present the average result for the peak 5-minute period.

Figure 7.2 Typical up-peak traffic template (15% handling capacity)

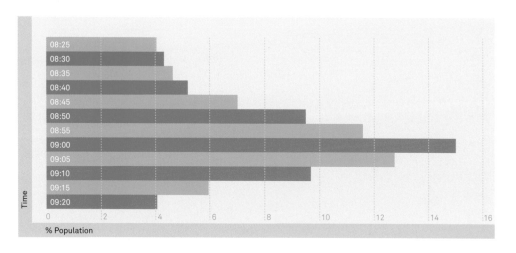

7.1.3

The MRL lift maintenance panel usually located adjacent to the doors at the top floor can often be relocated to an alternative floor or a room adjacent to the lift well.

OTHER PASSENGER LIFT TYPES

Machine-roomless (MRL) lifts

Machine-roomless (MRL) lifts should be considered for use in buildings up to 85 m in height and operating at rated speeds up to 2.5 m/s. (Some commercial restriction on suppliers may exist at the higher travel and speeds.)

However, consideration should be given to the fact that the inherent design characteristics of these lifts requires certain maintenance and modernisation activities to be carried out from the lift lobbies.

The MRL lift maintenance panel usually located adjacent to the doors at the top floor can often be relocated to an alternative floor or a room adjacent to the lift well.

MRL lifts must be capable of release from safety gear operation under power without the need for specialised equipment.

Lifts for tall buildings
Lifts for tall buildings should always be designed in conjunction with specialist advice.

→ Consider the use of sky lobbies and express shuttles when number of floors exceeds 35–40
→ Consider the use of double-deck lifts and other technologies
→ Include a passenger rescue strategy for express zones.

It is not practical to include escalator travel time when calculating time to destination in double-deck systems.

7.1.4

RIDE QUALITY AND NOISE LEVELS

The ride quality of passenger lifts should be measured using appropriate calibrated precision-grade vibration and sound recording equipment fitted with the latest software.

A series of measurements needs to be made following the general methodology of BS ISO 18738: 2003 over different journeys in both directions of travel, including: a full height run; a run over approximately half travel; and a number of single floor journeys.

All measurements should be taken over a full lift cycle, defined as a single journey starting when the lift doors commence closing on one floor to the point when they are fully open on the destination floor. The noise and maximum peak-to-peak measurements should demonstrate compliance with the following criteria when measured at 1 m from the lift door or shaft wall as appropriate.

The maximum vibration levels measured on the floor slabs in occupied office areas shall not exceed a Vibration Dose Value (VDV), as defined in BS 6472-1: 2008, of 0.36 m/s$^{1.75}$ during an 8 hour working day (equivalent to 0.4 m/s$^{1.75}$ for 16 hours).

Table 7.1 Noise levels for lifts

Maximum noise level	
In lift car	55 $L_{Amax (fast)}$
In lift lobby	55 $L_{Amax (fast)}$
Into offices without lift lobbies	50 $L_{Amax (fast)}$
Into offices through lift shaft walls	35 $L_{Amax (fast)}$

Note: The maximum noise values specified above shall be measured with any in-car mechanical ventilation devices switched both 'on' and 'off'.

Table 7.2 Vibration levels for lifts

Maximum vibration level	
Horizontal vibration	0.12 m/sec^2 (12 mg)
Vertical vibration	0.15 m/sec^2 (15 mg)
Maximum acceleration	1.2 m/sec^2
Maximum jerk	1.8 m/sec^3

Note: The maximum vibration values specified above are the peak-to-peak levels using the ISO ride quality filter.

7.1.5

£ In larger buildings with multiple firefighting lifts, consider combining one of the firefighting lifts with one of the main passenger lifts in a through-car arrangement (subject to building control approval).

FIRE FIGHTING LIFTS

Fire fighting lifts are provided adjacent to fire fighting stairs, constituting a fire fighting shaft. These are provided for new buildings over 18 m in height, and are designed specifically to assist fire fighters access the upper floors in larger buildings. The design of the overall shaft is governed by BS 9999. The requirements are very specific and should be considered early in the process. Although the lifts cannot be used for transporting goods, there is the potential for executive or staff use, especially from basement car parks.

7.1.6

GOODS LIFTS

Goods lifts should be provided in buildings over 10,000 m² NIA and carefully considered for buildings over 5,000 m² NIA. With large floor plates, consideration should be given to accessing the goods lift to facilitate efficient sub-division of the floor plates. For buildings over 25,000 m², consider a second goods lift.

The link to the loading bay needs to be direct and provide easy access to sufficient storage space for sorting and recycling materials.

Goods lifts should:
→ Be provided for general use, with consideration of clean and dirty building operation
→ Be sized for plant replacement and full-height partition panels (provide service to all roof and basement plant levels where possible)
→ Be accessible from all potential occupier demises
→ Be fitted with durable finishes (e.g. stainless steel); if any finish is susceptible to damage, an appropriate means of protection should be provided.

Even when there is no dedicated goods lift, lift size and access to allow transportation of furniture and fit out materials should be reviewed at the design stage.

7.2

Consider the provision
of disabled access lifts
adjacent to the escalators.

ESCALATORS

Escalators are generally used in an office context to provide an enhanced vertical transportation service to the lower levels of a building, to deal with high traffic requirements due to dealer floors, auditoria or restaurants, and so on. They are also needed to service the upper deck level in double-deck lift installations and are sometimes used to deal with changes of level externally in the public realm areas.

Escalators should ideally be of 30-degree inclination and minimum 800 mm step width. 35-degree inclination machines may be considered where space constraints exist and where the vertical travel does not exceed 6 m.

The rated speed should be between 0.5 m/s and 0.65 m/s, depending upon vertical travel.

CARDINAL PLACE, LONDON
Courtesy of Otis Ltd

Design considerations:
→ Select the escalator to suit the application
→ Preferably have three flat steps at each landing and 1100 mm high balustrades for enhanced safety
→ Have 1000 mm wide steps, where associated with public circulation space, e.g. office retail podiums, external circulation applications, and so on
→ Provide energy-efficient features such as variable voltage, variable frequency machines, automatic slowdown/ full speed and LED lighting.

FURTHER READING
British Standard BS
5656 Part 2 *Code
of practice for the
selection, installation
and location of new
escalators and moving
walks,* BSi

RIDE QUALITY

The ride quality of escalators should be measured using specialist measuring equipment.

The results of the noise and maximum peak-to-peak vibration measurements, taken in accordance with the methodology of ISO/CD25744 with the escalator running in both directions, shall demonstrate compliance with the ride quality criteria set out in Table 7.3.

The maximum vibration levels measured on the floor slabs in occupied office areas shall not exceed 0.01 m/s^2 peak acceleration, based on Wb weighting, as defined in clause 3.3 of BS 6472-1, 2008.

Table 7.3 Noise and vibration data for escalators

Maximum noise and vibration	
Noise level at 1.5 m above any step or upper/lower landing level on any individual escalator	55 $L_{Amax(fast)}$
Vibration on step band	0.1 m/sec^2 (10 mg)
Vibration on handrail	0.35 m/sec^2 (35 mg)

Escalators are generally used in an office context to provide an enhanced vertical transportation service to the lower levels of a building, to deal with high traffic requirements due to dealer floors, auditoria or restaurants

DASHWOOD HOUSE, LONDON
Photographer: Paul Grundy

8.0 / ACOUS

Noise levels in an office affect the ability of occupants to concentrate and be productive. In extreme cases, excessive noise can be harmful to hearing and overall well-being. It is therefore essential to ensure that office designs provide adequate noise and vibration control measures, as described in this Section.

TICS

TALKING POINTS

Sustainability

Business performance

Cost & value

ACOUSTICS

8.0 / ACOUSTICS

8.1 SOURCES OF NOISE AND VIBRATION

The acoustic environment inside an office building depends on the perceived level of noise and vibration from:

→ Externally generated sources, such as local road traffic; nearby over/underground train movements and aircraft flyovers
→ Internally generated building services plant and equipment
→ Occupational sources, such as occupant operations and office equipment
→ The degree of acoustic separation afforded by internal walls and floor slabs.

The design of noise and vibration control measures in occupied office areas should take account not only of the building structure, but also the surface finishes likely to be used by future occupants of the building. The 'confidentiality' or 'privacy' levels that may be required between adjacent cellular spaces such as offices and meeting rooms, etc. is an important design feature.

8.2 DESIGN CRITERIA

For general open-plan offices, floor to ceiling height should not exceed 3 metres and should have high sound absorption (e.g. 0.9 averaged over the frequency range 500 Hz to 2000 Hz). Floors should be carpeted in office areas and adjacent circulation spaces.

Relaxations of the internal and external criteria are normally acceptable for emergency or standby plant, but should comply with local authority requirements, occupational requirements and not interfere with internal audible emergency alarms.

8.2.1

EXTERNAL NOISE INTRUSION

External noise intrusion levels (whether from road, rail or aircraft sources) should, after attenuation by the composite building envelope, not exceed the following acoustic design criteria when measured under Cat A standards (including carpets), in accordance with the Association of Noise Consultants Guidelines ANC-9801:1998 – Part 2: *Noise from External Sources (e.g. traffic noise) within buildings.*

Open plan offices:	NR40 (L_{eq})
Speculative offices:	NR38 (L_{eq})
Cellular offices:	NR35 (L_{eq})

(Note: The speculative office criterion is a compromise between the ideals for open plan and cellular offices.)

In addition, $L_{Amax(fast)}$ noise intrusion levels should not normally exceed 55 dBA in open plan/speculative offices or 50 dBA in cellular offices. In the case of naturally ventilated buildings, it may be appropriate or necessary to accept higher external noise intrusion levels than shown above (e.g. +5 dBA relaxation in maximum ventilation mode provided occupants have the choice). Measures to minimise the impact of rainfall noise should be considered.

8.2.2

INTERNAL NOISE

Sound level difference vertically between individual office floors should be at least $D_{nT,w}$ 45 dB at shell and core stage, or at least $D_{nT,w}$ 48 dB if fitted to Cat A standards when tested in accordance with BS EN ISO 140-4: 1998 and rated in accordance with BS EN 717-1: 1997. Where mock-up rooms are used for testing, they should have a floor area not greater than 20 m^2 to ensure that the sound field is uniform.

Flanking transmission horizontally across cladding mullions at potential fit-out partitions should be capable of demonstrating a weighted normalised flanking level difference of at least $D_{nF,w}$ 45 dB when tested in a laboratory in general accordance with EN ISO 10848-2: 2006 and rated in accordance with BS EN ISO 717-1: 1997. Flanking constructions should be capable of being upgraded in the (Cat B) fit-out up to at least $D_{nF,w}$ 53 dB.

The degree of privacy between spaces will be determined by the levels of masking noise and the internal sound insulation between partitioned areas. Internal partitions that form part of the occupier fit-out are discussed further in detail in *BCO Fit-Out Guide:* Section D7. However, where an adjacent office occupier demise is separated by a wall constructed as part of the shell and core or Cat A fit-out, then the same sound insulation standards as set for the floors shall be achieved.

8.2.3

VIBRATION

Vibration transfer from continuous sources (e.g. plant items) to internal areas should not exceed 0.01 m/s² peak acceleration, based on Wb weighting as defined in clause 3.3 of BS 6472-1: 2008. Vibration transfer from intermittent sources (e.g. underground trains) to internal areas should not lead to re-radiated noise level in occupied cellular offices and meeting rooms in excess of 45 $L_{Amax(fast)}$, or in the case of open plan offices in excess of 50 $L_{Amax(fast)}$.

Lift and escalator noise and vibration criteria, including within the lift car, lift lobbies and adjacent office areas should be controlled to meet the requirements of Section 7 of this *BCO Guide to Specification.*

8.2.4

BUILDING SERVICES NOISE

Building services noise should be controlled to meet the following noise ratings (ref BS8233: 1999, Annexe B) when measured under Cat A standards in accordance with the Association of Noise Consultants guideline ANC 9701:1997- Part 1: *Noise from Building Services.*

Cellular offices:	NR35
Speculative offices:	NR38
Open plan offices:	NR40
Entrance lobbies:	NR40
Circulation spaces:	NR40
Toilets:	NR45
Loading bays:	NR55
Underground car parks:	NR55

Plant room noise levels should be designed to suit adjacent occupied areas and to comply with noise at work regulations. (See Appendix A2: Statutory regulations and Appendix A3: Health and safety.)

BREEAM Offices 2008 states that the combined noise levels shall not exceed 40 dB $L_{Aeq,T}$ (approximately NR34) in single occupancy offices and shall fall in the range 40–50 dB $L_{Aeq,T}$ (approximately NR34–44) in multi-occupancy offices. These criteria must be compared with the combination (i.e. sum) of the external noise intrusion and building services noise criteria above, not separately.

ACOUSTICS

The BREEAM requirement for multi-occupancy offices is consistent with BCO and other standards, although in a quiet office (e.g. served by a chilled beam or chilled ceiling system) electronically generated background 'pink/white' noise may need to be introduced to achieve BREEAM's lower noise limit. Unfortunately the BREEAM requirement for single occupancy offices is inconsistent with BCO, CIBSE and other industry standards. Adherence to the latest BREEAM proposals would result in reduced privacy between offices, or the need to up rate partitioning, due to lack of masking noise from building services which BREEAM would limit to somewhere in the range of NR25–34 (depending on contribution from traffic noise).

The above criteria, when coupled with the external noise intrusion levels (see 8.2.1, above) should show compliance with BS 8233: *1999 Sound Insulation and Noise Reduction for Buildings – Code of Practice.*

Building services plant external noise emission levels will need to comply with local planning/environmental authority requirements and statutory noise nuisance legislation.

For residential neighbours, all commercial services plant noise shall be at least 5 dBA lower (10 dBA if tonal) than the otherwise prevailing background noise L_{90} levels, when measured at a distance of 1 metre from the nearest noise sensitive window.

For commercial neighbours, 10 dBA below the internal building services noise level within the space should generally be acceptable.

OLD BROAD STREET, LONDON
Copyright: Hammerson

FINISHE
AND BU
COMPL

Early decisions about the level of fit-out, and careful preparation for completion and hand-over, make a considerable contribution towards the overall success and sustainability of an office building. This Section includes a useful checklist for issues that need to be addressed prior to completion.

S, FIT-OUT
LDING
ETION

TALKING POINTS

Sustainability

Business performance

Cost & value

9.1 DEFINITIONS

In a **'Shell and Core'** development:
→ The entrance hall, staircases, common/circulation areas, toilets, vertical transportation and cores will be fully furnished
→ Base build services plant and equipment will be terminated at breakout points to each floor
→ Life safety infrastructure (e.g. sprinkler pumps, tanks, risers, main fire alarm panel and emergency standby generator, etc.) will be installed
→ The finishes to the office face of core walls and finishes to the inside face of external walls and to columns should be of a level of finish ready to receive direct decoration.

Category A (Cat A) works essentially extend central services out onto floor plates and provide a background for Category B works. Category A works comprise services, life safety elements and basic fittings and finishes for the operation of lettable work space, including:

→ Suspended ceilings
→ Raised floors and skirtings
→ Cooling and heating systems
→ Office ventilation systems
→ Open plan base lighting solution
→ Life safety systems (fire alarms, sprinklers, emergency lighting, etc)
→ Distribution boards
→ Office carpet and floor boxes (usually in the form of a cash contribution to the occupier)
→ Blinds (can be either installed by the developer or a cash contribution made to the occupier)
→ Basic statutory signage
→ Basic security system and wireways.

Category B (Cat B) works, or bespoke fit-out, may include:

→ Suspended ceiling upgrades and special area fitting out (auditoria, kitchens, restaurants, meeting rooms, etc)
→ Upgrade to core finishes

It is often less expensive and more efficient for an incoming occupier to fit out a floor finished to Shell and Core standard than from Category A. This approach could reduce duplication of work and minimise waste.

→ Internal partitioning
→ Additional floor finishes
→ Mechanical, electrical services and lighting upgrade
→ Installation of below floor and overhead/ drop down power distribution
→ IT and telecommunications installations and distribution (data cabling)
→ Enhanced WC provision if required
→ Occupier standby generation and UPS
→ Adaptation of life safety systems
→ Decoration and branding
→ Fixtures and fittings
→ Furniture
→ Security installation enhancements
→ Audio/visual installation
→ Corporate and way finding signage
→ Vertical transportation enhancements
→ Feature staircase links between floors.

New speculative developments are usually completed to a Category A finish. This is primarily aimed at improving the marketability of a building.

Developments which have been pre-let off plan (or during construction if the programme is not too far advanced), are usually completed to Shell and Core. In this case, once the building is complete, the occupier will then undertake their own fit-out with a financial contribution from the developer for Category A elements.

However, since the change in empty rates regulations, the cost to the landlord in holding empty offices which are finished to Category A (rather than Shell and Core) has increased substantially. Many developers are now reappraising and changing their strategy on large speculative developments, with maybe one or two floors being completed to Category A for marketing purposes and the remainder to Shell and Core.

As part of a leasing transaction, the occupier's Category B works may be incorporated into the development programme and provide a 'turn key' fit out. The costs would be factored into the financial terms of any transaction.

9.0 /

9.2

Material selection should strike a balance between whole-life cost and environmental impact and consider opportunities for locally sourced, reclaimed and recycled materials. Materials should ideally achieve an 'A' rating in the BRE Green Guide to Sustainability.

FURTHER READING
The Impact of Office Design on Business Performance, BCO/ CABE Report, May 2005

9.2.1

For stone, consider sourcing material which is located locally to site. Transportation of stone over long distances will form the largest part of its impact on energy consumption.

Decoration specifications should be a balance of quality, robustness and environmental impact.

Fixtures, fittings and furniture including reception desks, shelving, storage cupboards and worktops are plant assets within the main pool for capital allowances.

FINISHES AND FIT-OUT

Finishes in all areas of the building should be fit for purpose. The office floor plate finishes are the back drop for a Cat B design and fit out by others.

Landlord's areas, reception, stairs, lifts and WCs should be designed using durable materials selected to ease maintenance but with some imagination that gives the building design individuality. Getting the design right has a profound effect on workplace productivity and business performance for future occupiers of the building.

MAIN RECEPTION

Reception areas need to respond to their function of welcoming and directing staff and visitors. The size and atmosphere should provide a space reflecting its transitional nature from outside to inside; and the space should use good quality materials. Flooring should provide a hard-wearing non-slip surface – materials such as natural stone and composite stone are ideal. Walls can be a combination of plasterboard with stone or other feature material highlights. Lighting will be key in providing the right environment.

1 KINGDOM STREET
Copyright: Sectorlight

9.0 /

9.2.2

STAIRS

Lighting and finishes should encourage people to utilise the stairs. Simple painted plasterboard to walls with self finish concrete soffits are acceptable. Treads of carpet, rubber or self finished concrete will suffice along with metal balustrades and handrails.

9.2.3

Lift lobbies should use hard-wearing, easy-to-clean materials. Floor finishes should use non-slip materials or carpets. Choice of materials, colour and texture should be used to aid navigation to and from the lifts for the visually impaired.

LIFT CARS AND LIFT LOBBIES

Lift car interiors are generally regarded as an integral part of the entrance hall design, and it is appropriate to carry the floor finish through into the lift car. Other finishes (and especially controls) should be selected from the manufacturer's standard range. Good quality wall finishes using mirrors, stainless steel and timber panelling are all available from these model ranges.

Lifts used for transporting goods require durable finishes, usually patinated stainless steel and vinyl flooring. Passenger lifts used for occasional goods use should be provided with an appropriate means of protection, such as hooks and drapes.

9.2.4

TOILETS AND SHOWER ROOMS

The selection of durable materials that will withstand the wet conditions is essential. Developers often use toilet areas as a branding opportunity, as well as providing a basic amenity for the building. Economy can be achieved by using conventional decoration to plasterboard away from wet areas.

Areas around urinals, wash hand basins and toilet pans should be finished with splash-resistant and easy-to-clean materials. Floors should be in a hard-wearing non-slip easily cleaned finish – usually natural stone or ceramic tiles. Floors generally work best with skirting of the same material. Module size is dictated by the size of the washroom area.

A myriad choice of wall, pedestal or vanity mounted basins is available; and all are equally acceptable as long as soap dispensing, towel dispensing and/or hand driers are catered for in the design.

Consideration should be given to the provision of lay-down areas for personal hygiene and cosmetic products, together with mirrors (part and/or full height) to cater for people working extended hours or preparing to attend after hours functions, etc.

Where unisex superloos are provided, particular attention should be paid to ensuring adequate sound insulation between cubicles.

133 HOUNDSDITCH, LONDON
Copyright: Will Pryce

9.2.5

OFFICE AREAS

Walls and doors
Core and column walls should be painted plasterboard with MDF or similar skirting and offer a clean and simple backdrop for economical Cat B fit outs. Doors to core areas can vary between good quality paint grade timber/metal and timber veneer.

Design concept, target market and rental level will inform the choice of finishes used on accommodation and riser access doors.

Doors often have to meet specific acoustic and fire integrity requirements, so these should be identified early in the process, together with interfaces for security access and key suiting.

Ceilings
Traditionally, good quality, modular perforated metal ceilings are preferred. They should be fully integrated with the space planning grid and provide a regular layout for luminaires, grilles, sprinklers and other services elements.

Raised floors
Medium-grade raised floors are recommended. They should achieve the following criteria:

→ Point load (over an area of 25 mm × 25 mm): 3.0 kN
→ Uniformly distributed load: 8 kN/m²
→ Air leakage (typically): 1.5 l/s/m² (based on floor at 25 Pa cavity pressure)
→ Fire performance: Class 0

Depending on the structural finish, there is an increasing opportunity to omit the ceilings, expose the soffit and suspend the services above the office space. This gains some environmental control benefit from the thermal mass, and works particularly well for multi-service chilled beam solutions.

£ £ Carpets, blinds and
curtains are eligible
plant items for tax relief
where they are installed and
paid for by the landlord or
through a capital contribution
to the occupier.

Strengthening could be considered to routes with heavy traffic, such as entry points and notional corridor routes. This will also be required in high load usage areas (computer rooms, roller racking, etc).

For areas immediately outside goods lifts, and any other areas identified by the client/occupier as requiring additional loading requirements, a suitable heavy-grade tile should be used. Computer rooms, telecommunications rooms and wiring closets will utilise anti-static, vinyl back, raised floor tiles.

Carpet

Carpet selection should aim for a combination of durability, quality and low static. The carpet should also achieve a recycled material content of at least 50%. Given the above, there is a wide range of choice for designers, with suppliers able to provide a multitude of design options at a cost effective price.

Ideally, office carpet should be A-rated as defined in the BRE *Green Guide to Specification*.

ISG ALDGATE HOUSE, LONDON
Photographer: Richard Leeney; Copyright: ISG

9.0 /

9.3 BUILDING COMPLETION

The completion of a building is usually a time of heightened activity, as various parties look to conclude their contractual obligations to each other. From a construction perspective, the works undertaken during this period often set the tone of future relationships or the perceived quality of the end product. Either way, this is a critical period that needs to be considered in due time and managed accordingly.

The key documents and issues that should be considered at the completion of a building construction project are discussed below.

9.3.1 BUILDING CONTRACT

Most forms of building contract provide for a definition of completion for a project. This is often known as 'practical completion'.

The term 'practical' can often be misleading, because it suggests that less than fully complete may be acceptable. This depends entirely on the drafting of the contract and the level of discretion provided to those administering it. As such, great care should be taken to fully understand the obligations imposed on the parties.

The building contract may also state specific items that must be provided before practical completion may be granted. Such items may include collateral warranties, specific documentation, spares and tools, and so on.

£ Interaction with occupiers
is important as there
may be tax issues associated
with lease incentives, such as
contributions and rent-free
periods. Failure to plan properly
can result in tax leakage.

Agreement for lease

If a pre-let has been secured, an 'agreement for lease' will be
in place. Such agreements typically include provision for the
occupier to make representations to the contract administrator
at handover inspections. It is essential that all parties
understand these key documents and their obligations and look
to work in a collaborative manner to gain a completion that all
are satisfied with.

Other agreements

There are, of course, a myriad of other agreements that are
relevant at completion, such as a lease agreement if the site is
leasehold, development agreements, funding agreements, etc.
Again, due consideration needs to be given to any completion
criteria or obligations that are given so that proper discharge
may be gained and documented.

9.3.2

STATUTORY OBLIGATIONS AND HEALTH AND SAFETY

A completed building will need to be compliant with the relevant
statutory requirements, such as planning and building control.
As completion approaches, these items need to be monitored
closely and managed so that the relevant approvals are achieved
and recorded in a timely manner.

Due consideration needs to be given to the condition the building
will be in at completion, and how this impacts on any statutory
compliance. For example, a building that is complete only to shell
and core will receive approval only to this state.

The Construction (Design Management) Regulations 2007 for
notifiable projects only, places a duty on clients, designers,
principal contractors, other contractors and CDM Co-ordinators
to provide information for the Health and Safety File, which must
be issued to the client at the end of the construction phase of
the project.

FURTHER READING
See Appendices A2:
Statutory regulations
and A3: Health and
safety.

This file should contain all the information needed to allow future construction work, fit-out, cleaning, maintenance, alteration, refurbishment and demolition to be carried out safely. It is likely in practice that the health and safety file will cross-reference to the operation and maintenance manuals. The content and accuracy of this information requires careful review as part of the completion process. This information may not be in its final form but must be sufficient to discharge the above obligations.

9.3.3

FURTHER READING
CIBSE Commissioning
Codes and BSRIA
Commissioning Guides
Building Regulations
Part L 2006 edition

BRE Digest 474,
*HOBO Protocol,
Handover of Office
Building Operations*
(incorporating March
2003 amendment)

BRE Digest 478,
*Building Performance
Feedback: Getting
started*

BCO Fit-Out Guide
sections D10.6
and E2.5

RIBA *Commercial
Offices Handbook,*
2003

COMMISSIONING AND HANDOVER

Building services systems need to be commissioned before they are handed over as complete. This may take a considerable length of time and an adequate period should be allowed in the construction programme. Individual systems are commissioned first and then the entire installations subjected to integrated systems testing to demonstrate that they work as a whole.

Integrated systems testing should demonstrate how the building will work under 'real life' conditions, simulating normal operations and emergencies:

→ Normal operation commissioning proves that the building can be kept functional and comfortable within the design criteria.
→ Emergency operation scenario testing proves that the building can function safely under life safety conditions, e.g. during a fire or a mains power failure.
→ A 'doomsday' test exposes the building's systems to extreme conditions and proves that they can cope and recover to the design conditions.

Frequently, an occupier will appoint an independent validation engineer to witness commissioning and confirm that design conditions can be achieved. This is particularly important where a building is being taken as shell and core only, because an occupier will rely on base building systems to provide the primary services needed for his fit out.

The commissioning process should include training of the facilities management staff so that they are able to take safe control of the building immediately on handover. Operation and maintenance manuals, record information, and as-fitted drawings should be provided at the same time to assist them in the operation and maintenance of all systems.

A poorly managed building can quickly offset the benefits of an energy-efficient design. It is therefore essential that the final occupants of the building are familiar with the systems.

A non-technical guide explaining the operation of the building and its engineering systems should be prepared and provided to each occupier. This is to allow the building users to get the best from the systems provided. BREEAM Offices 2008 gives guidance on requirements for building user guides.

The provision of good-quality, user-friendly information, to both the building operators and occupants, is a key component for delivering a sustainable building. CIBSE TM31: *Building Log Book Toolkit* provides guidance and templates that allow designers and contractors to communicate key components of design intent, construction quality and commissioning records to the building operators. BREEAM Office credit M12: Building User Guide (along with a similar credit for BREEAM Retail) provides an outline of what this sort of guidance must contain in order to achieve the BREEAM credit. For each topic, BREEAM requires that appropriate guidance be provided to the facilities manager (such as how to operate the central HVAC controls, change set points, etc.), and to the occupants (such as how to operate whatever controls they are given locally for their portion of the building).

FURTHER READING
CIBSE TM31: Building *Log Book Toolkit*, 2006, available www.cibse.org

BREEAM Office 2006, Assessor Manual, credit M12: Building User Guide; at www.breeam.org

Post-completion building
evaluations once the
building is occupied are useful
to determine, if issues arise,
whether they are buildings-
related or user-related. Building
evaluations can help to inform a
users action plan for on-going
energy and water reduction
measures.

During the first year of occupation, the occupier or building operator should measure the performance of the building services and use the information gathered to fine-tune the systems, maximising the energy saving potential of the design. This process is particularly important where low and zero carbon systems have been used.

Procedures for preventative measures against the sludge-generating effects in pipework of the aerobic bacteria, pseudomonas, should be incorporated into the commissioning documentation.

9.3.4

GOOD PRACTICE AND GENERAL CHECKLIST

A smooth completion is driven by preparation and common agreement on standards and expectations. The following should assist the process:

→ A schedule of regular inspections prior to final completion with the key parties
→ Phased sign-offs so that elements or areas of the building are agreed as finished prior to completion
→ Inspections of elements and areas before they are covered up
→ A dry-run of completion so that all parties are familiar with the process
→ A well-planned and managed commissioning strategy.

£ Design intent and cost data are essential to support an auditable maximised capital allowances claim. O&M manuals are critical in identifying ECA qualifying assets.

The following should be considered prior to the award of practical completion. Please note that this list is for guidance only, it is not exhaustive and the exact contents will be informed by the above and the completeness of the building (i.e. Shell and Core, Cat A or Cat B, etc).

→ Air leakage test
→ Asset registers
→ 'Black Building or Doomsday Testing' complete
→ Cleanliness – inside and externally
→ Completion of services commissioning regime
→ Cradle, lift and escalator testing
→ Defects list and clearance programme (if applicable)
→ Earth bonding
→ Electrical testing
→ Emergency lighting
→ Energy performance certificate (EPC)
→ Envelope testing – air pressure, water, impact, etc
→ Environmental testing periods
→ Health and safety file
→ Insurances
→ Life safety systems
→ NIA/ GIA final area measure and confirmation
→ O&M manuals and 'as built' drawings
→ Service meter readings
→ Services 'cause and effect' testing
→ Sprinkler systems
→ Statutory approvals
→ Tools, spares and keys
→ Training for facilities staff
→ Water systems/quality

APPEN

DICES

A1

Consider mechanical elements of gates, bollards and barriers as qualifying machinery for capital allowances tax relief.

FURTHER READING
BCO Security Guide 2009

Copyright: Sutton Young

SAFETY, SECURITY AND RISK

Office buildings and their occupants can be at risk from many forms of crime, ranging from vandalism, crimes against the person, petty theft, organised crime, industrial espionage, civil disruption and terrorism.

The response to mitigate these risks needs to be appropriate and proportionate, and will depend on many factors including location and occupier profile. Planning for security in the built environment, like planning for business, should be wide ranging and inclusive. The employer's duty of care makes this an essential task for any business. In addition, corporate governance requires a full analysis of business continuity to be undertaken and disaster recovery plans to be agreed and put in place.

The optimal approach should consider the full spectrum of potential events as part of a comprehensive risk assessment from natural disasters and catastrophic events (such as the attack on the World Trade Centre on September 11 2001), to events such as anti-global protests and recurring events such as petty and serious crime.

Risk is not just the threat of outside attack, but covers internal operations that affect the location of key elements of the building such as the loading bay, plant areas, comms/data rooms etc. the location of these all need to be considered, in relation to personnel security and business resilience from the outset.

The process illustrated in Figure A1.1 can be used to organise a building project in order to respond to potential risk. Detailed support information can be found in the forthcoming BCO Security Guide 2009.

Figure A1.1 Developing a security strategy

PROCESS   OPTIONS

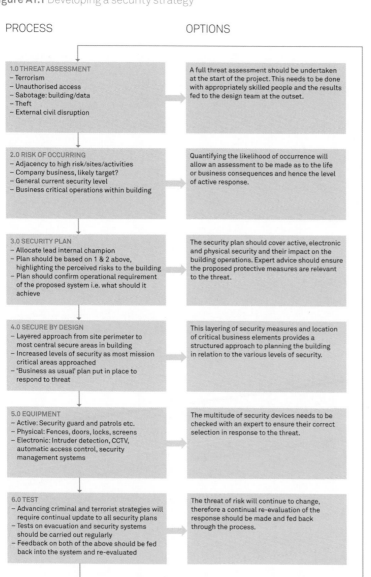

1.0 THREAT ASSESSMENT
– Terrorism
– Unauthorised access
– Sabotage: building/data
– Theft
– External civil disruption

A full threat assessment should be undertaken at the start of the project. This needs to be done with appropriately skilled people and the results fed to the design team at the outset.

2.0 RISK OF OCCURRING
– Adjacency to high risk/sites/activities
– Company business, likely target?
– General current security level
– Business critical operations within building

Quantifying the likelihood of occurrence will allow an assessment to be made as to the life or business consequences and hence the level of active response.

3.0 SECURITY PLAN
– Allocate lead internal champion
– Plan should be based on 1 & 2 above, highlighting the perceived risks to the building
– Plan should confirm operational requirement of the proposed system i.e. what should it achieve

The security plan should cover active, electronic and physical security and their impact on the building operations. Expert advice should ensure the proposed protective measures are relevant to the threat.

4.0 SECURE BY DESIGN
– Layered approach from site perimeter to most central secure areas in building
– Increased levels of security as most mission critical areas approached
– 'Business as usual' plan put in place to respond to threat

This layering of security measures and location of critical business elements provides a structured approach to planning the building in relation to the various levels of security.

5.0 EQUIPMENT
– Active: Security guard and patrols etc.
– Physical: Fences, doors, locks, screens
– Electronic: Intruder detection, CCTV, automatic access control, security management systems

The multitude of security devices needs to be checked with an expert to ensure their correct selection in response to the threat.

6.0 TEST
– Advancing criminal and terrorist strategies will require continual update to all security plans
– Tests on evacuation and security systems should be carried out regularly
– Feedback on both of the above should be fed back into the system and re-evaluated

The threat of risk will continue to change, therefore a continual re-evaluation of the response should be made and fed back through the process.

RE-EVALUATE

A2 ▬▬▬▬▬

STATUTORY REGULATIONS

The Building Regulations in England and Wales and Northern Ireland, together with the Scottish Building Standards exist to ensure:

→ The health and safety of people in and around buildings
→ The conservation of fuel and power
→ Accessibility for people with disabilities.

In addition, these regulations are being updated to include sustainability and security. Consequently, protecting the environment and enhancing sustainability will increasingly become binding requirements of these Regulations.

Designers are at liberty to demonstrate compliance with the requirements of these regulations using parameters other than those contained in the Approved Documents – in England and Wales (ADs), Technical Booklets in Northern Ireland (TBs) and Technical Handbooks in Scotland (THs). Fire engineering, for example, is an accepted alternative method to achieve the requirements of AD:B, TB:E and TH:2.

There are two ways in which to obtain approval for a project under the Building Regulations in England and Wales. The first is by applying to the relevant local authority (LA), the second is to engage an approved inspector (AI).

Local Authority (LA) planners offer the choice of 'Full Plans' approval or 'Conditional' approval. 'Full Plans' requires all documents to be submitted to the LA, after which they have 35 working days to give a decision. More complex projects are usually processed using the 'Conditional' approval method. Sufficient information is submitted to the LA which then offers a 'Conditional Approval' stating what those conditions may be. Sufficient information is often General Arrangement plans, sections and elevations and supporting documents to indicate the fire strategy (AD:B), accessibility (AD:M), toilet provision (AD:G) and energy consumption (AD:L) of the building. The Conditional Approval will require all other matters to be agreed as the design progresses.

Approved Inspectors are engaged by the client as part of the design team and notify the LA that they have been appointed. They then advise and approve the plans and the work on site, notifying the LA when everything has been completed satisfactorily.

A2.1

MEANS OF ESCAPE (AD:B, TB:E AND TH:2)

A new British Standard BS 9999: *Fire Safety in the Design, Construction and Use of Buildings* was published at the end of 2008. This replaces most of the sections of BS 5588 and provides tables and calculations to assist in applying the principles of Fire Engineering. Technical guidance is provided to allow flexibility in design and fire risk management. BS 9999 replaces DD (Discussion Document) 9999, which has been around for a few years and which many Building Control personnel had already been accepting as an alternative approach to achieving the requirements of AD:B, TB:E and TH:2.

A2.1.1 Occupation densities

Occupation densities are relevant to BS 9999 and AD:B, AD:M/ TB:E, TB:R/TH:2. Despite the findings of various studies into the average occupation densities of office buildings, AD:B for example still requires escape provisions to be calculated on a density of 6 m^2 per person. However, different densities can be the subject of negotiation with the building control officer or approved inspector. This should be done at the earliest opportunity in the design process.

BS 9999 allows flexibility of design when set against the provision of Automatic Fire Alarm Systems and Sprinklers. By determining the risk profile of the building, the following criteria may be adjusted to achieve greater efficiency:

→ Maximum direct distances: 12 m where travel is possible in one direction only; 30 m where travel is possible in more than one direction
→ Maximum travel distance: 18 m where travel is possible in one direction only; 45 m where travel is possible in more than one direction
→ Travel distance in dead end condition
→ Alternative escape routes
→ Widths of escape routes and exits
→ Widths of stairs
→ Fire fighting stairs and lifts.

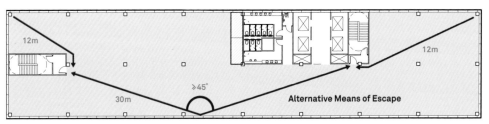

Courtesy of Sheppard Robson

A2.2

TOILET ACCOMMODATION (AD:G)

When British Standard 6465: 2006 was published, it required a greater provision of toilet facilities in offices than were referred to in BS 6465: 1994 and 1984 – the Standards that are currently (2008) cross-referenced in AD:G 1992. These anomalies are being addressed.

A new edition of AD:G is expected in 2009 which will refer to the latest version of BS 6465. This is also under review and an addendum is to be published in 2009 to address the issues raised by the industry, including:

→ Reference to fire escape density for toilet planning to be removed
→ Recommended density of 1 person per 10 m^2 and 60/60 split
→ Calculations on a floor by floor basis only, not whole building
→ Numbers of fittings for male and female rationalised
→ BS 6465: 2006 allows the inclusion of fully accessible self-contained cubicles in the calculations, whereas previous editions did not.

Toilet accommodation is also discussed in terms of accessibility in AD:M Section 5 Clauses 5.5 to 5.21, which explains the size and layout of a fully accessible WC cubicle. Note that:

→ Clause 5.7c is a requirement that at least one WC cubicle is provided in separate-sex toilet accommodation for use by ambulant disabled people
→ Clause 5.7d states that, where there are four or more cubicles in separate-sex toilet accommodation, one of these must be an enlarged cubicle for use by people who need extra space, in addition to any provision under Clause 5.7c.

However, some building control officers and approved inspectors will accept the omission of some of these provisions if an adjacent fully accessible toilet cubicle is available. The reader should check TB:R for similar requirements. The Scottish Standards do not have a separate section for access by people with disabilities. These requirements are contained, where relevant, in all sections of the Handbooks.

Further details on toilet provisions are given in Section 3.3 Building form: Core elements.

A2.3

ACCESS TO AND USE OF BUILDINGS (AD:M AND TB:R)

Access to and use of buildings is covered by AD:M and TB:R. These cross-refer to British Standard 8300: 2001 which contains more detailed information. The latter is currently under review and an updated version is planned.

The key topics covering office buildings in AD:M are:

→ Disabled parking bays: 3.6 m wide × 6.0 m long (note: the access zone around a standard parking bay has to be outside any carriageways or vehicular routes)
→ External ramped access: described in AD:M Clauses 1.19 to 1.26
→ External stepped access: described in AD:M Clauses 1.27 to 1.33 (note: where there appears to be a conflict between the guidance in part M and Part K, Part M takes precedence)
→ Internal ramps – AD:M Clauses 3.52 and 3.53
→ Internal stairs – AD:M Clauses 3.50 and 3.51 (note: the number of risers per flight is limited to 12, and the dimensions of each riser should be between 150 mm and 170 mm)

Design requirements for staircases take into account the special needs of ambulant disabled people. The requirements apply to all staircases. Early negotiation with the building control officer or approved inspector may allow some relaxation on certain features of accommodation stairs if compliant stairs and lifts are located close by.

A2.4

CONSERVATION OF FUEL AND POWER
(AD:L, TB:F, TH:6)

Approved Documents L1A, L1B, L2A, L2B came into force in England and Wales on 6 April 2006. Carbon emissions are the key driver and the documents are in line with the European Energy Performance of Buildings Directive. The measures require new buildings to have a specified reduction in carbon emissions when compared with the requirements that they would have had under the 2002 edition of AD:L. The reader should check TB:F and TH:6 for similar updates.

A2.5

FUTURE PUBLICATIONS

The whole structure of the Building Regulations: England and Wales is currently under review. Proposals include a review of selected Approved Documents on a three yearly basis, and self-certification by professionals.

Approved Document G: Hygiene: It is proposed to re-issue this document in 2009. Changes that are proposed include (but are not limited to):

→ Provision of water divided into 'wholesome and non-wholesome' categories
→ Co-ordination with Water Company by-laws
→ Limitation on water quantity provision on a person/day basis
→ Control of temperature for hot water at taps
→ Updated co-ordination with current standards (e.g. BS 6465: 2006).

Approved Document L Conservation of Fuel and Power: It is proposed to re-issue this document in 2010. Changes that are proposed include (but are not limited to):

→ Co-ordination with new legislation
→ Correct errors in the 2006 edition
→ Update to incorporate advice on new technologies.

BS 8300: 2001: Design of buildings and their approaches to meet the needs of disabled people. Code of Practice: A new revised and updated version of this standard was available for public consultation until 31 July 2008. It is expected that the new version will be published in 2009.

A3

HEALTH AND SAFETY

In addition to the Building Regulations, other legislation and/or guidance relating to health and safety includes the following (note: reader to check that the version consulted is the current version):

The Construction (Design and Management) Regulations: 2007.

Managing Health and Safety in Construction
Approved Code of Practice and Guidance on CDM Regulations 2007.

The Management of Health and Safety at Work Regulations 1999, (re-printed February 2005)
Management of Health and Safety at Work – Approved Code of Practice and Guidance 2001.

Workplace (Health, Safety and Welfare) Regulations 1992 (amended 1995)
Workplace health, safety and welfare – Approved Code of Practice 2002.

Provision and use of Work Equipment Regulations 1998
Safe use of work equipment – Approved Code of Practice and Guidance 2001.

Health and Safety (Display Screen Equipment) Regulations (amended 2002)
Work with display screen equipment – guidance on regulations 2003.

Manual Handling Operations Regulations 1992 (as amended)
Manual handling – guidance on regulations 2004.

Personal Protective Equipment at Work Regulations 1992
Personal protective equipment at work – guidance on regulations 1993.

A3.1

THE CONSTRUCTION (DESIGN AND MANAGEMENT) REGULATIONS: 2007

The CDM Regulations were originally published in 1994 and substantially revised in 2007. They are primarily about the management of health and safety in the design, construction, use of, and eventually demolition of, buildings.

These regulations are intended to bridge the gaps that existed between the design, construction and maintenance of buildings. They placed duties on Clients, Designers and Principal Contractors, and their sub-contractors, and created a new duty holder now called the CDM Co-ordinator (CDMC). All have shared responsibilities to plan, co-ordinate, and manage health and safety through all the stages of a construction project.

The CDM Regulations were originally published in 1994 and substantially revised in 2007.

Most of the main changes in these regulations are now well established. One important provision to note is that the client is responsible for appointing the CDM Co-ordinator and until such time as the appointment is made, the client automatically assumes the responsibilities of the CDMC.

There is a greater emphasis on hazard identification and risk reduction. The Health and Safety Executive remains keen to reduce the amount of 'paper trail risk assessments', which it considers to be of little use, unless the risk reduction related to that assessment is incorporated into the design.

An important change in CDM: 2007 is the incorporation of requirements from the Management of Health and Safety at Work Regulations. Designers of workplaces must therefore design to reduce risks to users as well as those involved in construction, maintenance and demolition activities.

THE BROADGATE TOWER (PLAZA AND GALLERIA), LONDON
Courtesy of British Land. Photographer: Richard Leenery

A4

MIXED USE: TECHNICAL ISSUES

A4.1

STRUCTURAL GRIDS

Grid design is of particular importance if the building is a horizontally divided mixed-use building, for instance, if the structural grid is driven by car parking. Depending on the nature of the mixed use there may be an argument to use a grid dimension of 7.5 m (three parking bays) by 15 m for offices and residential.

Compromises in column position in car parking bays can achieve significant savings by reducing the span of the transfer structure at the office or residential level. Generally speaking supermarkets are largely the most grid-sensitive use and it is easiest, structurally, to assume the following mixes.

→ Residential over retail over car parking
→ Residential over offices over non-food retail
   (car parking separate)
→ Offices over retail over car parking.

This is not an exhaustive list, but represents those uses where the structure can be economically resolved. Although structural steel is often the preferred form of office and retail construction, it needs to be carefully considered for use in residential, because it can be complicated and more difficult to resolve acoustic issues.

For all structural solutions, industry cost bench-marking standards have to be intelligently applied, because mixed use structures are inevitably more complicated than single use structures.

A4.2	SERVICES

The clear benefit of the integration of different uses is that, subject to the mix, there is a good case for site-wide service provision. Depending on the load balance between the different use types, a mixed use development can often be ideal for an 'energy centre' solution using combined heating and power (CHP) plant or combined cooling, heating and power (CCHP) plant.

There is inevitably the requirement for the separation of services to the various uses for reasons of both access and metering. One of the advantages of the large and somewhat inevitable structural transfer structure, is that it provides a natural zone for horizontal distribution, thus helping with this separation.

A4.3	PARKING

Parking is without doubt the single most complex issue; made more complex by the layering of uses.

Assuming that the mixed use model in question is a complex, high density and essentially urban one, then the site may well benefit from high levels of public transport provision. Although this may well be accepted as the norm by office developers it does little to reduce retailers' requirements, especially those selling food and consumer goods. These same urban constraints will tend to suggest that there is pressure to make part or all of the car parking subterranean – with clear cost consequences.

Despite the obvious architectural consequences there is a strong case for parking above and below active ground floor uses in order to minimise excavation.

Although there is some shift in shoppers' and retailers' perception, it may be a long time before car parking is significantly reduced in retail-led schemes.

A4.4

ACCESS

The general desire of developers is to create separate access (principally cores) for each use. This inevitably leads to duplication and a poor net-to-gross floor area ratio.

There is mixed experience with both local authorities and fire engineering consultants as to what level of sharing there can be, however the following combinations have been made to work in the past.

→ **Residential over offices.** Shared use of goods lift subject to adequate security controls.

→ **Shared means of escape (stairs) subject to security controls.** Use of one of the residential lifts as fire fighting access to offices subject to the lift being in a separate shaft and the residential also being serviced by a goods hoist.

CARDINAL PLACE COURTESY OF LAND SECURITIES
Photographer: Paul Grundy

A5

BUSINESS PERFORMANCE

A5.1

ENHANCING BUSINESS PERFORMANCE FOR A
DIVERSE WORKFORCE

FURTHER READING
Welcoming Workplace,
RCA, 2008

*The Impact of Office
Design on Business
Performance,* BCO/
CABE, 2005

Creating a productive environment for an increasingly diverse
and multi-generational workforce is set to become a growing
priority in office design.

This is because of the changing age balance of the working
population – we are now beginning to see four generations at
work in one open plan office. While there has been much focus on
Generation Y (i.e. people born between 1977 and 1995) and their
expectations as they enter the workforce, the real demographic
shift is in the growing numbers of older workers who will not
retire, but will remain at work for longer, many of them on a
consultancy, special-project or part-time basis.

Several factors are driving this trend: a shortfall in pension
funds; a management emphasis on retaining knowledge and
experience built up over years; age and disability discrimination
legislation offering more protection to older workers; and, above
all, the fundamental demographic facts of population ageing –
one in two adults in the European Union will be over 50 by 2020.
But if working lives are to be extended, workplaces will need to
flex and adapt to help the people who want to keep on working.

Leading organisations place high value on the individuals who
perform 'knowledge work'. The attraction and development of
talented staff has become a priority, and this will increasingly
extend to the retention of highly experienced, older staff
who, in many cases, represent the repository of a company's
tacit knowledge.

There are a number of key issues to consider with respect to
office buildings for an ageing workforce in the knowledge
economy, as the Royal College of Art's Welcoming Workplace
study (2007/08) revealed. Led by the Royal College of Art, Helen
Hamlyn Centre, and funded jointly by the EPSRC and AHRC under

the 'Designing for the 21st Century' initiative, this study investigated 'knowledge workers' in the UK, Japan and Australia.

The broad trend in office design has been towards open plan working. While current workspace design serves many of the collaborative aspects of knowledge work well, for some, including many older knowledge workers, this has been at the expense of space for concentrated work. 'Solo' knowledge work is particularly compromised by background noise. As a result, many workers seek alternative environments, such as taking tasks home when they need to concentrate. Meeting and social spaces offer no respite from the communal life of the office. By redressing the balance between collaboration and concentration, by promoting the recuperative qualities of space for contemplation, and by recognising the limitations of hot-desking, office design would address the issue of 'institutional ambivalence' towards older workers while making the total environment more productive for everyone.

A5.2

FURTHER READING
'Indoor Climate and Productivity in Offices and How to Integrate Productivity in Life Cycle Cost Analysis of Buildings Services' by Wargocki et al, in Federation of European Heating and Air-conditioning Association (REHVA) Guidebook No 6, ISBN 2-9600468-5-4, 2006

Clements-Croome D. J., *Creating the Productive Workplace*, Second edition. Routledge, 2005

INDOOR AIR QUALITY AND BUSINESS PERFORMANCE

Improved air quality can be generated by the use of 'green' design, building materials and technologies which decreased the risk of building sickness syndrome and other infections such as influenza and various allergies. The wider indoor environment of the building incorporates colours, space and workstation design; indoor air quality and climate covering the thermal conditions, cleanliness as well as the movement of indoor air; lighting in terms of quality and quantity; acoustics in terms of sound level and speech intelligibility. Various research indicates that short term sickness leave, performance of call centre operators in particular tasks such as text typing and proof reading can improve significantly when the ventilation rates rise from 3 l/s per person to 24 l/s per person.

Poor air quality leads to poor performance, due to distraction by odour, sensory irritation, allergic reactions or direct toxicological effects. It is also important, however, to have a very strict maintenance regime to ensure that all of the equipment including filters are cleaned or replaced on a regular basis.

QUANTIFYING THE EFFECT OF BUILDING PERFORMANCE ON
BUSINESS PERFORMANCE

Proper commissioning of M&E systems, plus continuous/
seasonal commissioning once the building is occupied, is an
essential part of providing a healthy work environment. The cost
of continuous/seasonal commissioning is small when compared
with the energy and maintenance cost savings it brings to the
building in operation.

Once occupied, the building's energy consumption tells a lot
about how the building is performing, making the provision
of good, clear energy information an important tool for the
facilities manager (FM). Information about the fuels used in
the building – namely half-hourly electricity and natural gas
(or other heating fuel) – should be provided in a simple, clear
format so that the FM can see at any given time how much
energy is being used in each tenancy, or each zone within a
tenancy, of a multi-occupied building.

There are a number of indoor environmental quality (IEQ) factors
which may be measured, to ensure a comfortable, productive
environment is provided to the occupants. These include:

→ Space temperature
→ Relative humidity (RH)
→ Lux on the working plane
→ Metabolic carbon dioxide (generated by breathing)
→ Volatile organic compounds (VOCs).

FURTHER READING
Clements-Croome,
D.J., et al, *High-Quality
Building Services based
on Whole Life Value*,
University of Reading,
School of Construction
Management &
Engineering, December
2006

These items may be measured via fixed sensors for permanent monitoring, hand-held equipment for spot checks, or data loggers for longer-term measurement.

The next generation of data loggers will allow low-cost monitoring of indoor environmental parameters once the building is occupied. These data loggers have many uses, and may be dotted around the building – for example, as part of a continuous commissioning exercise to verify the temperatures or RH values that fixed sensors are sending back to the BEMS.

Another innovative use of modern technology is the use of wireless sensor networks to collect 'real time' occupant data, producing a dynamic picture of building performance in use. These sensors are worn by a representative sample of building occupants, and measure heat flux across the wearers' skin, measuring thermal comfort, skin conductivity, measuring physical exertion and emotional response to stimuli such as stress, the body's core temperature, and an accelerometer to measure motion.

A6

FURTHER READING
*BCO Guide to Green
Incentives*, 2009

TAXATION

Since the last BCO Guide to Specification was published in 2005, significant changes have been made to the treatment of capital assets in the UK and in particular to the capital allowances systems. The changes have been driven by the increasing use of green technologies, sustainability measures and the broader reform of corporation tax.

This Appendix provides an overview of the capital allowances system and how it may apply to the development of office space for owner occupation or investment purposes. Although each taxpayer will have numerous other factors to take into account, there are a number of areas within the legislation which could impact on the overall tax position where due consideration should be given.

A6.1

CAPITAL ALLOWANCES

A significant proportion of the expenditure on an office building can qualify for tax relief through capital allowances.

The cashflow benefit is obtained by means of a reduction in a building owner's liability to tax on business profits or rental income. The qualifying assets – 'plant and machinery' – are predominantly (but not exclusively), linked to the services installations, cladding system and furniture, fitting and equipment elements. The expenditure broadly falls into three categories – integral features; main pool; and enhanced capital allowances (ECAs) – as set out in Table A6.1.

Qualifying plant and machinery assets are not defined per se within the capital allowances legislation, but rather through a series of broad guidelines backed up by particular tests and precedent case law dating back to the late 19th century. Eligibility is determined by such factors as the nature of the asset, the purpose and degree of fixing and the particular business use to which the asset is put by the taxpayer. Table A6.2 shows the type and ranges of expenditure that may qualify for allowances.

Table A6.1 Capital allowances

Category	Rate*	Notes
Integral features	10%	Heating, ventilation and air-conditioning installations, cold water systems, electrical systems, lift installations, external solar shading
Main pool	20%	Welfare facilities, finishings, furniture and fittings, fire detection and fire fighting installations, telephone and data systems, particular machinery and equipment
Enhanced capital allowances (ECAs)	100%	Energy and water-saving plant and machinery from approved lists

*The rates relate to the annual writing-down allowance (WDA) claimed on a reducing balance basis for expenditure incurred after April 2008.

When considering assets qualifying for 100% relief under the ECA regime, reference must be made to the approved energy-saving and water-conserving technologies listed on the ECA website managed by The Carbon Trust on behalf of DEFRA (www.eca.gov.uk). The full relief can only be claimed in the year of expenditure, although it can also be converted to a credit of 19% where the taxpayer may not be able to immediately benefit from the relief.

Where assets are leased to occupiers, the impact of the long funding lease legislation requires the landlord to assess which assets are deemed to be 'background' plant, basically the 'ordinary' assets within an office building. Assets installed which are not 'background' must be tested further to determine whether they are within certain minimis limits.

It is important to note that not all building owners can benefit from capital allowances. For example, REITs (see below) and pension funds will not pay tax (although REITs have a shadow capital allowances regime); and property traders are taxed differently, but they may benefit indirectly in some cases.

For those owners and investors who are able to utilise the allowances, planning and professional advice is essential, particularly given the increasing complexity of the system against a backdrop of self-assessment compliance.

Proactive tax planning for capital allowances throughout the development period will potentially provide greater benefit than a retrospective claim.

Table A6.2 Qualifying expenditure types

Expenditure type	Range	Key factors
Shell and Core	25% to 30%	M&E services, vertical transportation and façade engineering will impact on the range
Fit-out	Up to 80%	Services, finishings, voice and data installations and landlord-adopted occupier enhancements. Consider impact on levels of non-background plant under Long Funding Lease legislation
Refurbishments	30% to 50%	Incidental structural alterations, consider repair elements too
Contributions	Max 100%	Critical on how any lease incentive is structured

Figure A6.1: Advantages of tax planning: The additional capital allowances benefit obtained through proactive tax planning during the development period, as compared with expected levels for a retrospective claim post-completion

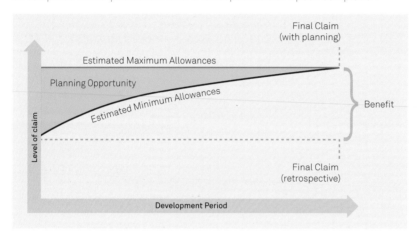

A6.2

REAL ESTATE INVESTMENT TRUSTS (REITs)

Real Estate Investment Trusts (REITs) came into effect in the UK on 1 January 2007. While these are primarily tax-exempt vehicles for owning property, they are required to operate within a shadow capital allowances regime.

The shadow capital allowances regime is mandatory. The maximum amount available must be taken into account when calculating the tax exempt profits and the REIT will have no discretion or opt out. Shareholders receive a distribution from the profits of the tax-exempt business after deduction of capital allowances. There are no provisions that allow shareholders to directly access capital allowances on tax-exempt business assets.

The issue is important because one of the key conditions applying to a REIT is that at least 90% of the profits of the tax exempt business must be distributed to shareholders. Capital allowances are 'automatically' taken into account in calculating the profits and so have the effect of reducing the minimum distribution. A REIT does not have a choice as to whether it claims allowances or not. The maximum allowances available (be they first year or writing down allowances) must be taken into account in computing profits.

A6.3

LAND REMEDIATION RELIEF

Additional tax relief is available for UK companies remediating contaminated land. The relief allows a company to claim 150% of the total cost of remediating a contaminated site, including preliminaries and associated professional fees. Not all 'remediation costs' qualify; only those costs incurred as a direct consequence of contaminated materials being present on the site. There are a number of complex entitlement and eligibility conditions and specialist advice should be sought if remediation costs are envisaged.

For successful applicants however, the relief can provide a valuable cash contribution to the remediation costs. The significance of the contribution will depend on the amount of qualifying spend and the status of the claimant. For a developer, the tax relief is claimed in the year of sale and is worth 14% of the cost of qualifying works. An investor, on the other hand, can claim the relief in the year that the expenditure is incurred and this offers a significant cash benefit in the early stages of a project.

Restrictions apply in that the claimant company cannot be (or connected with) the original polluter; the works should not be subsidised or qualify for capital allowances. Where the relief creates a loss, then the company may either carry forward the loss or claim a tax credit by surrendering any unrelieved losses for a payment equal to 16% of the loss surrendered.

A7

LOW AND ZERO CARBON TECHNOLOGIES

LZC FUEL /TECHNOLOGY	DESCRIPTION/COMMENTS	ADVANTAGES
Solar water heating	Solar thermal panels use sunlight to heat water. For most commercial applications, panels are made from a series of evacuated tube collectors. Other types of system use flat-plate collectors (domestic) or unglazed plastic collectors (swimming pools).	Solar hot water heating has similar advantages to those of photovoltaics, although solar hot water panels are less costly.
Photovoltaics (PV)	Photovoltaic (PV) panels contain many thin wafers of silicon that have been manufactured to produce electricity when exposed to sunlight. An array of PV panels will generate DC electricity that is passed through inverters to produce AC electricity, which can be used by the building. Any surplus electricity may be fed back into the National Grid.	Photovoltaic panels are a very flexible renewable energy option because they can be specified and installed at relatively late stages of a project. They affect building architecture to a lesser extent than other renewable energy technologies and usually do not involve an arduous permitting process (cf. wind turbines, biomass, or open-loop ground source heat pumps).
Combined heat and power (CHP)	CHP systems use an engine-driven alternator to generate electricity and use the waste heat produced by the engine, jacket and exhaust to provide heating and hot water.	CHP systems generate electricity and heat locally, thus eliminating transmission losses associated with conventional electricity networks. In office developments, CHP systems can be designed to supply excess heat to nearby residential units, healthcare, or leisure facilities.

LIMITATIONS	CARBON SAVINGS	COST EFFECTIVENESS*	APPLICABILITY TO OFFICES
To be financially viable, the building will generally have a year-round demand for hot water. The panels should be installed on a portion of the building, typically the roof, which faces south or southwest.	Medium * Useful only for domestic hot water, therefore not much benefit for normal office use.	Medium	Medium Unlikely to be viable in small offices, viability increases where kitchens and showers are provided.
The PV panels should be located on a portion of the building, typically the roof, which faces south or southwest. PVs are generally one of the most expensive options for renewable energy generation.	Low relative to high cost * Typically savings will not exceed 1%.	Low However, costs are predicted to improve.	Low to Medium Low carbon savings for cost means that greater savings could be found with other technologies. Can be effective where solar shading is replaced with PVs.
For CHP to be considered financially viable, it would generally need to operate at least 4,500 hours per year. In a typical office the greatest demand is for cooling rather than heating. CHP is only viable if there are other uses for the heat, such as would be found in a mixed use development or where chilling equipment can be driven efficiently from the heat generated by the CHP unit.	Medium Can be improved if biomass fuel is used.* Load profile of an office alone is unsuitable for CHP.	Medium Requires full utilisation of waste heat.	Low to Medium Depends on finding a use for the waste heat. High if a good load balance can be found to utilise the waste heat e.g. as part of a mixed use development.

*From Illustrated Guide to Renewable Technology, BSRIA 2008

LZC FUEL /TECHNOLOGY	DESCRIPTION/COMMENTS	ADVANTAGES
Biomass heating	Examples of biomass fuels include wood chips, wood pellets and energy crops such as those used to produce biodiesel.	Biomass heating can meet 100% of the building's heating demand. The technology is easily integrated into current solutions in building services engineering and conventional ventilation, and cooling strategies may be used in conjunction with biomass heating.
Fuel cells	A fuel cell is an electrochemical conversion device. In principle, it operates like a battery, but it does not run down or need to be recharged. As long as a fuel is supplied, a fuel cell will generate electricity and produce heat and water as by-products.	The waste heat can be harnessed in the same way as CHP. Hydrocarbons are used as fuels, e.g. natural gas, alcohol and hydrogen. If hydrogen can be provided from a renewable source, then the fuel cell has no carbon emissions.
Biomass CHP	Biomass CHP uses a biomass fuel to power a CHP engine.	See advantages for biomass and CHP.
Groundwater abstraction – open loop providing cooling only	Water is abstracted from an aquifer via boreholes and used to provide heating or cooling in the building before being reintroduced to the ground.	The water is at a stable temperature throughout the year and offers much higher heat transfer than ground source heat pumps.

LIMITATIONS	CARBON SAVINGS	COST EFFECTIVENESS*	APPLICABILITY TO OFFICES
Delivery and storage of fuel on site should be considered at an early stage of the design. The delivery vehicle will often require space to make a 3-point turn. Recent questions concerning the sustainability and reliability of fuel supply makes biomass heating a renewable energy option that requires careful and thorough research.	Medium A biomass boiler could reduce carbon emissions by about 10%	Medium More expensive than conventional boilers.	Low to Medium Unlikely to be viable in city centre locations where fuel delivery, storage space and air pollution will be a problem. Space take up can affect viability. Maintenance intensive.
Heavy and expensive. The technology is immature for building applications. Until hydrogen is available from a piped network, fossil fuels in the form of natural gas must be used.	Medium Depends on full utilisation of generated heat and fuel source * See reductions for CHP.	Low Limited range of commercially available fuel cells, and expensive.	Low to Medium Future advances in technology or infrastructure may make fuel cells more viable.
See disadvantages for biomass and CHP. The technology is in the very early stages of development for small building scale systems.	Medium to High Load profile of an office alone is unsuitable for CHP.	Medium Requires full utilisation of waste heat.	Low to Medium Depends upon usage of heat. Unlikely to be viable in city centre locations where fuel delivery, storage space and air pollution will be a problem.
There are usually onerous licence conditions and the boreholes may not behave as predicted, leaving shortfalls in heating and cooling capacity.	Medium * Where heating and cooling energy is balanced.	Medium Depends on the cost of boreholes.	Medium Depends upon choice of cooling system in the building.

*From *Illustrated Guide to Renewable Technology*, BSRIA 2008

LZC FUEL /TECHNOLOGY	DESCRIPTION/COMMENTS	ADVANTAGES
Ground source heat pumps (GSHP) – closed loop providing heating and cooling	Heat can be dumped into the ground when a building needs cooling and extracted when heating is needed. The driving force for the heat transfer is provided by a heat pump. Pipework is buried in the ground, frequently as part of the foundation construction and is often embedded in the piles.	The ground stable temperature allows the heat pump to run at favourable operating conditions throughout the year.
Wind turbines	A wind turbine is a machine with rotating blades that converts the wind's kinetic energy into rotary mechanical energy, which in turn drives a generator to produce power.	Wind turbines provide very clean renewable energy at lower cost than many other renewable energy options and may be the ideal choice in remote locations.
Trigeneration – Combined Cooling Heat and Power (CCHP)	Trigeneration consists of a CHP plant linked to an absorption water chiller. Waste heat from the CHP plant can be used either for heating or to produce cooling.	Trigeneration extends the hours of operation of a CHP plant and improves the financial viability.

LIMITATIONS	CARBON SAVINGS	COST EFFECTIVENESS*	APPLICABILITY TO OFFICES
The capacity of the heat pump is limited by the amount of ground available for heat transfer. A small footprint restricts the heating and cooling that can be provided.	Medium High Coefficients of Performance (CoPs) are dependant on relatively low supply temperatures for the heating system.* Where heating and cooling energy is balanced.	Medium	Medium Depends upon site conditions and design of heating and cooling systems.
The predicted average wind speed for the proposed site should be above 3.5 m/s for small turbines and 6 m/s for large ones. Because of planning restrictions and turbulence, large wind turbines are generally not a viable option for urban office schemes.	Low to medium Large sized turbines in non-urban or off-shore locations will be more effective.* Small machines on the roof may only achieve about 1% reduction in carbon emissions.	Low Depends greatly on available wind conditions. Actual power output likely to be much less than rated output.	Low
Depending on the fuel used, may be more carbon intensive than a combination of a high efficiency gas boiler and conventional water chiller. Absorption chillers do not respond well to changing load patterns.	Medium to high* However, this depends upon the figures used to assess the comparison with a conventional system.	Medium High initial cost and specialised maintenance	Medium Load patterns need to be assessed and carbon savings accurately assessed before committing to the relatively large investment.

*From *Illustrated Guide to Renewable Technology*, BSRIA 2008

A8   OPTIONS FOR CONTROLLING THE INDOOR ENVIRONMENT

FOUR PIPE FAN COIL

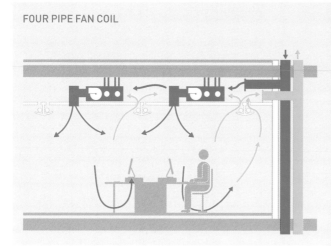

ADVANTAGES
→ Good temperature control
→ High cooling capacity
→ Good flexibility/adaptability
→ Individual control possible
→ Widely known and understood

DISADVANTAGES
→ Noise level can be high
→ Energy efficiency average
→ Maintenance costs high – regular access required to the ceiling void
→ Risks of leaks from condensate pipework in false ceilings

VARIABLE REFRIGERANT FLOW/VOLUME (VRF/VRV)

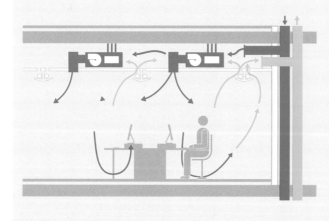

ADVANTAGES
→ Good temperature control
→ Good flexibility/adaptability
→ Individual control
→ Modular, proprietary system, easy to install

DISADVANTAGES
→ Noise level can be high
→ Maintenance cost high – regular access required to ceiling void to clean filters etc.
→ Risks of refrigerant leakage from pipe work in false ceiling
→ Limitations on refrigerant pipe work length and height difference between indoor and outdoor units
→ Risks of leaks from condensate pipework in false ceilings

VENTILATED CHILLED BEAMS

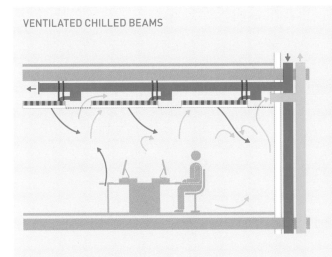

ADVANTAGES

→ Good temperature control
→ Very low noise level
→ Moderate to high cooling capacity
→ Individual control possible
→ Energy efficiency good
→ Maintenance costs moderate

DISADVANTAGES

→ Flexibility/adaption can be restricted – careful consideration required during fit out (partitioning)
→ Condensation risk – supply air normally dehumidified and chilled water temperature elevated

VARIABLE AIR VOLUME SYSTEM (VAV)

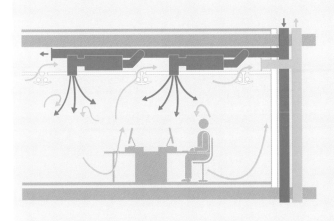

ADVANTAGES

→ Good temperature control
→ Low noise level (higher for fan-assisted VAV)
→ High cooling capacity
→ Reasonable flexibility/adaptability
→ Individual control possible
→ Energy efficiency can be high at part load conditions and benefits from 'free cooling'

DISADVANTAGES

→ Maintenance costs average to high (high for fan-assisted)
→ Potential problem with air dumping at high downturn ratio
→ Possible outdoor air starvation at low load conditions
→ Large plantrooms, ceiling and riser voids required

CHILLED CEILING

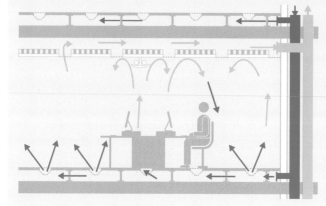

ADVANTAGES

→ Good temperature control
→ High level of comfort due to radiant heat exchange
→ Very low noise level
→ Energy efficiency good
→ Maintenance costs average

DISADVANTAGES

→ Moderate to low cooling capacity
→ Flexibility/adaptability can be limited
→ Individual control not normally required
→ Condensation risk – supply air normally dehumidified and chilled water temperature elevated

DISPLACEMENT VENTILATION

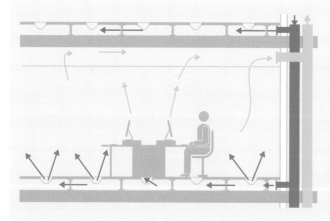

ADVANTAGES

→ Reasonable temperature control
→ Very low noise level
→ Energy efficiency good – significant free cooling
→ Maintenance costs low
→ Good indoor air quality due to direct removal of contaminants from space

DISADVANTAGES

→ Specialist floors required
→ Low cooling capacity – often used with chilled ceilings or passive chilled beams
→ Restricted flexibility/adaptability – location to terminal devices needs to suit furniture layouts
→ Individual control not generally possible
→ Large terminals may take up wall/floor space
→ Enhanced floor to ceiling height required (preferably not less than 3 m)

NATURAL VENTILATION

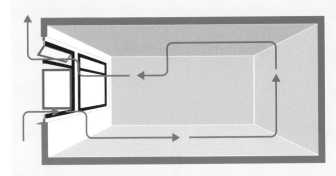

ADVANTAGES
→ Minimum energy use
→ Maintenance costs very low
→ Simple to operate

DISADVANTAGES
→ Poor temperature control
→ Possible noise and pollution (including pollen) problems from openings
→ Very low cooling capacity
→ Poor flexibility/adaptability – cellularisation will restrict air flow paths

Based on original images courtesy of Battle McCarthy

257

		Section
OCCUPANCY		
Workplace density (NIA per workspace)	8–13 m²	3.2
Means of escape (NIA per person)	6 m²	3.2
Core elements (NIA per person)	12 m²	3.2
On floor services (NIA per workspace)	10 m²	3.2
PLAN EFFICIENCY NIA:GIA		
Low rise buildings (up to 9 floors)	80–85%	3.8
PLAN DEPTH AND CEILING HEIGHT		
Deep plan:		
Window to window (or atrium)	15–21 m	3.1.1
Window to core	6–12 m	3.1.1
Finished floor to underside of ceiling	2.6–2.75 m	3.1.1
Shallow plan:		
Window to window	12–15 m	3.1.2
Window to core	6–7.5 m	3.1.2
Finished floor to underside of ceiling	2.6–3.0 m	3.1.2
GRIDS		
Planning grid	1.5 m × 1.5 m	3.6.1
Column grid	7.5 m, 9.0 m and 12.0 m	3.6.2
CIRCULATION		
Percentage of primary circulation to NIA	15% to 22%	3.7

		Section
TOILET PROVISION		
NIA per person	12 m²	3.3.3
Male/ female ratio	60%/60%	3.3.3
Unisex	100%	3.3.3
LIFTS		
Performance requirements:		
Car loading	80% (60–70% scenic)	7.1.1/7.1.2
Waiting time	< 25 seconds	7.1.1/7.1.2
Handling capacity (up-peak)	15%	7.1.1/7.1.2
Handling capacity (two-way lunchtime)	12%	7.1.1/7.1.2
NIA per person	12m²	7.1.3
Hall call systems:		
Time to destination	< 90 seconds (up to 15 floors)	7.1.2
RAISED FLOORS		
Typical floors	150 mm (overall)	6.3
Trading floors	300–500 mm (overall)	6.3
STRUCTURAL LOADING		
Live:		
Ground floor and below ground office floors	3.0 kN/m²	6.1.1
Above ground	2.5 kN/m²	6.1.1
High load areas (over approx 5% of floor area)	7.5 kN/m²	6.1.1
Dead:		
Partitions	0.5–1.2 kN/m²	6.1.1
Floors, ceilings and services equipment	0.85 kN/m²	6.1.1

		Section
SMALL POWER		
On floor distribution (based on 1 workspace per 10 m²)	25 W/m²	6.2.1
Diversified load (over 1000 m²)	15 W/m²	6.2.1
LIGHTING		
Daylighting (target)	2% average; 0.8% minimum	6.2.2
Average maintained illuminance:		
VDU use	300–500 lux	6.2.4
Paper based tasks	500 lux	6.2.4
Task uniformity	0.7	6.2.4
Unified glare rating (UGR)	19	6.2.4
Electrical load allowance	12 W/m² (incl. task lighting and Cat B allowance)	6.2.4
Lighting energy use	15–30 kWhr/m²/year	6.2.4
COMFORT		
Airtightness	Not more than 3.5 m³/hr/m² for building at 50 Pa	5.4.1
Outdoor air	12–16 l/s per person	6.2.2
Occupancy	1 workspace per 10m²	6.2.1
Air conditioned space:		
Summer	24°C ± 2°C	6.2.2
Winter	20°C ± 2°C	6.2.2
Mixed mode/ natural vent:		
Summer	Not to exceed 25°C for more than 5% of occupied hours. Not to exceed 28°C for more than 1% of occupied hours	6.2.2
Winter	20°C ± 2°C	6.2.2

		Section
NOISE CRITERIA		
External noise intrusion:		
Open plan	NR40 (L_{eq})	8.2.1
Speculative	NR38 (L_{eq})	8.2.1
Cellular offices	NR35 (L_{eq})	8.2.1
Building services:		
Open plan	NR40	8.2.4
Speculative	NR38	8.2.4
Cellular offices	NR35	8.2.4
SUSTAINABILITY		
BREEAM rating for new and refurbished offices	Minimum: 'Very Good'	
	Best practice: 'Excellent'	4.3.1

EDITORS:
Neil Pennell (Land Securities)
Geoff Harris (Henderson Global Investors)

COORDINATOR:
Clare Raven (Land Securities)

ARCHITECTURE:
Mark Dillon (Sheppard Robson)
Paul Sandilands (Lifschutz Davidson Sandilands)
Bob Keenan (Sheppard Robson)
Charles Bell (Keppie Design)
David Lawrence (Hamilton Associates)
Despina Katsikakis (DEGW)
Gary Rawlings (Make)
Gavin Murgatroyd (Gardiner & Theobald)
Jonathan Wilson (Carey Jones)
Murray Levinson (Squire & Partners)
Simon Laird (Simon Laird Associates)
Tim Fyles (Fletcher Priest)
Alex Wraight (Allies & Morrison)
Tim Williams (BDP)
Martin Sagar (Sheppard Robson)

COST & VALUE:
Nick Clare (Davis Langdon)
Peter Harrison (Davis Langdon)
Simon Rawlinson (Davis Langdon)
Paul Farey (Davis Langdon)
Bulen Hourshid (Davis Langdon)
Gavin Murgatroyd (Gardiner & Theobald)
Philip Esper (Davis Langdon)

WORKPLACE PRODUCTIVITY:
Ellen Salazar (ES Research & Consulting)
Derek Clements-Croome (University of Reading)
Eszter Gulacsy (MTT Sustain)
Jeremy Myerson (Royal College of Art)
John F. Smith (JSA Architecture Limited)
Philip Ross (Cordless Group)
Robert McLean (PricewaterhouseCoopers)
Paul Edwards (Hammerson)
Mike Jaggs (BRE)
Ken Giannini (MCM Architecture)
Jacqui Harrington

VERTICAL TRANSPORTATION:
Neil Pennell (Land Securities)
Adam Scott (Roger Preston)
Bill Evans (D2E International)
Simon Russett (Hoare Lea)
Julian Olley (Arup)

SERVICES:
Peter Williams (Arup)
Fiona Goddard (Aecom)
Iain Trent (Land Securities)
Stuart Morgan (Hann Tucker)
Tony Mayo (Hilson Moran)
Bulen Hourshid (Davis Langdon)
Rob Newman (IPT Design)
Nick Offer (Arup)
Giovanni Festa (WSP Group)
Mark Gellaitry (Blackwood Partnership)
Nigel Clark (Hilson Moran)
Paul Tremble (WSP Group)

STRUCTURES:
Paula Walsh (Arup)
Hanif Kara (Adams Kara Taylor)
Paul Scott (Adams Kara Taylor)
Philip Esper (Davis Langdon)
Glyn Trippick (Buro Happold)
Alex Wong (Waterman Group)
Richard White (Arup)
Cecilia Bagenholm (Buro Happold)
Michael Willford (Arup)
Adam Pearce (Arup)

ENVELOPE:
Edith Mueller (Arup)
Steve Mudie (Davis Langdon)
Will Stevens (Ramboll Whitby Bird)

SUSTAINABILITY:
Ant Wilson (AECOM)
Charles Bell (Keppie Design)
Mark Stewart (TP Bennett)
Gary Rawlings (Make Architects)
Ann Bodkin
Mark Dillon (Sheppard Robson)
Alex Amato (Davis Langdon)
Eszter Gulacsy (MTT Sustain)
Ellen Salazar (ES Research & Consulting)
Bulen Hourshid (Mott Green Wall)
Nick Cullen (Hoare Lea)
Paul Edwards (Hammerson)

PEER GROUP REVIEW MEMBERS:
Nick Ridley, President of the BCO 2008-2009, (NCReal Estate Consulting)
Mike Beaven (Arup)
Gary Wingrove (BT)
Paul Warner (3D Reid)
Carl Potter (GVA Grimley)
Cameron Stott (JLL)
Ian Cowley (Hoare Lea)
Martin Pease (Atkins)
Mat Oakley (Savills)
Grant Brooker (Foster + Partners)
Lee Polisano (KPF)
Paul Morrell (Davis Langdon)
Ron German (Stanhope)
Mark Whitby (Ramboll Whitby Bird)
David Long (Long & Partners)
Geoff Taylor (Land Securities)
David Farebrother (Land Securities)
Simon Forrester (Association of Interior Specialists)
Paul Harrington (PricewaterhouseCoopers and Corenet)

DRIVERS FOR CHANGE:
Geoff Harris (Henderson Global Investors)
Mark Dillon (Sheppard Robson)
Eszter Gulacsy (MTT Sustain)
Nick Williams (Savills)
Simon Rawlinson (Davis Langdon)

BCO SECRETARIAT:
Jenny MacDonnell (BCO)
Fiona Thomson (BCO)

Design by 300million

Endorsed by

CoreNet GLOBAL | UK Chapter